Shift
Your
Brilliance

HARNESS THE POWER OF YOU, INC.

SIMON T. BAILEY

Credits

Editor: DL Karl, Word Paper Scissors, Orlando, FL

Contributing Editor: Ellena Balkom, Written On Purpose, Savannah, GA

Caroline Bartholomew, Nashville, TN

Copy Editors: Lynette M. Smith, All My Best, Yorba Linda, CA

Lynette Majer: Lynette Majer LLC, San Francisco, CA

Sound Wisdom

P.O. Box 310

Shippensburg, PA 17257-0310

Previously published as *The Vujá dé Moment* by Dream Tree Productions Previous ISBN: 978-0972552004

For more information on foreign distribution, call 717-530-2122. Reach us on the Internet: www.soundwisdom.com.

ISBN 13 TP: 978-0-7684-0457-9

ISBN 13 Ebook: 978-0-7684-0458-6

For Worldwide Distribution, Printed in the U.S.A.

1 2 3 4 5 6 7 8 /18 17 16 15 14

CONTENTS

THIS BOOK IS FOR YOU

Are you ready to take your life to another level? Are you, your organization, or business overwhelmed by the shifts in the market, stressed to meet the demands of the emerging economy, or looking for the new breakthrough? Do you dread hearing the alarm go off on Monday mornings? Do you hit a mental snooze button and pretend all the depressing news in the world is just a bad dream? You're not alone. Research tells us that optimism is on the wane due to tough economic times and fears about the future.

This book is for people like you and me, who want to shift toward more positive thinking and are ready to work to create a better future for ourselves. It's for all of us who seek to make significant changes in our personal and professional lives and are determined to harness our own power. It's for the business leaders, managers, and employees who know they need to step up and become agents of change and creativity in today's challenging work environment and volatile marketplace. In this book, I believe you will find inspiration, insight, and concrete guidance that will allow you to make necessary, exciting, and long-lasting shifts of brilliance in both your personal and working lives.

INTRODUCTION

When I was growing up in Buffalo, New York, my parents enrolled me in a parochial school when I was just learning to talk. Yes, I do remember it. The nuns at this Catholic school were very strict. During this time they had my parents' permission to reintroduce the board of education to my seat of understanding. In other words, the paddle would become my best friend forever. Eventually I got a clue that the nuns were not putting up with my behavior, and I settled down. That early discipline became etched in my mind, as I began to matriculate through elementary and middle school.

As I prepared to enter the seventh grade, my parents made a seemingly abrupt decision to move me from St. James Catholic School to P.S. (Public School) #68. This new school was across the street from our new house. This sudden shift caused me to question what was happening to me. I had plans to make up stories as to why I was late getting home from school. Yes, even back then, I was strategically planning how to have fun without my parents knowing it. I survived the culture shock of transitioning from Catholic school to public school and then proceeded to high school.

In Buffalo, during that time, you could pick which high school you wanted to attend, and you were not restricted to only attending a school in your zip code. My parents chose for me to go to McKinley Vocational High School, which was named after William McKinley, the 25th President of the United States who was assassinated a few short steps from the site of the school. During the 1980s, each student at McKinley was expected to take vocational trade classes in sheet metal, carpentry, plumbing, and air conditioning. I am not sure why they wanted us to take an air conditioning class in the snow capitol of the world, but oh well, we went with it.

My first year of high school was bad. I failed all of the trade classes. My parents thought that since my dad could build anything with his hands, I would follow in his footsteps. Trust me, the genes for constructing are not in my DNA. As if flunking these classes wasn't enough, I went out for the football team and was cut. I tried out for the basketball team and was also dismissed as it was evident I was no Magic Johnson. Track and Field looked promising, however, when they saw how slow I was, the coaches suggested that maybe cross-country was a better fit. I think they felt sorry for me. I felt sorry for me, because I was attempting to force fit my way into a place in which I didn't belong.

Can you imagine the mental and emotional damage that was happening to me in my first year of high school? Dr. Carol Dweck, author of *Mindset—The New Psychology of Success* says, "In one world, failure is about having a setback. Getting a bad grade. Losing a tournament. Getting fired. Getting rejected. It means you're not smart or talented. In the other world, failure is about not growing. Not reaching for the things you value. It means you're not fulfilling your potential." My parents decided to shift me away from that environment where I was underachieving and seemingly unenthused about education. They knew that I had brilliant potential and needed to shift me into a more conducive setting where my talents—like running my mouth!—could be nurtured and appreciated. So, Mom and Dad enrolled me in Bennett High School, which I attended from my sophomore year through my senior year. It was at Bennett that I met my saving grace in the form of Ms. Rita Lankes, who taught English and became my favorite teacher. She truly understood that education was meant to polish and shape a diamond in the rough.

Well, you are probably wondering what happened in my last three years of high school. By the time I graduated, I was the senior class president. At Bennett High School, I found my voice. I found my fit. I found where I belonged.

Florence Shinn, the author of *The Game of Life and How to Play It* (published in 1925), makes this powerful statement, *"The thing man seeks is seeking him—the telephone was seeking the bell."* When I read this, all of sudden it clicked. In my first year of high school I was seeking something that *wasn't* seeking me. I needed to let go of failure and open up to what wanted to emerge, and more importantly, what belonged to me.

In other words, what you want, wants you.

It is my belief that we as human beings are pre-wired to be brilliant, but we settle for being less than audacious because of the micro-messages that we receive on a daily basis.

When I first wrote this book, the original title was *The Vujá dé Moment*. However, the more I lived, listened, and leaned in to what was happening globally and locally, I recognized that people and businesses everywhere from Atlanta to Australia, Los Angeles to London, Sioux Falls to Singapore were shifting and transforming.

Traveling the globe for my business allowed me to experience some exquisite moments that left an imprint on my psyche.

I experienced one of those moments while sharing the stage with the late Dr. Stephen Covey, author of *7 Habits of Highly Effective People*, and Libby Sartain, who was then Chief People Officer for Yahoo.com. That day Dr. Covey said, "We are not human beings having a spiritual experience, but we are spirit beings have a human experience." I had never heard a statement like this before. It is as riveting today as it was when he first said it.

I've chewed on that statement for nine years, and "bam," I had an Emeril Lagasse moment, and it finally hit me again. When you understand the science of your spirit, how you are wired, what makes you tick and click, then you realize you were created in brilliance to be audacious. The posture and disposition of audacious living is to possess a daring attitude of confidence with a high disregard for conformity, conventional thinking, or common existence.

As spiritual beings, we exist in a matrix, or quantum field, that is pulling things toward us like a magnet. We repel from us the things that are incongruent with our worldview. In other words, you will always attract people, situations, and circumstances based on the vibrational energy that you release into the universe through daily conversation. Please note that this book is not a remix of *The Secret*. I am just making a point. Audacious men and women are bold in their beliefs and convictions. That's why they are revered and admired in the matrix—because they have found a way to channel their energy like a laser in the direction of their intended destiny. They become iconic brands; think of people like Bono, Oprah, and the late Steve Jobs.

Audacious individuals have bought into the "as if" school of thought first introduced by William James (1842-1910), the one-time Harvard Professor of Anatomy, Psychology, and Philosophy. In his words, the idea behind the "as if" principle is, "Be not afraid of life. Believe that life is worth living, and your belief will help create the fact, and if you want a quality, act as if you already had it." WOW...that is so amazing. In the personal development field of the past, people have been taught to believe, behave, and then receive. However, audacious people who are committed to living brilliantly understand that you behave first, and then your beliefs catch up to the person you are becoming.

As you begin to comprehend the science of how your spirit functions as an audacious being, you realize that you are not trying to work your way toward the future; your future is already present.

The world-renowned Napoleon Hill said, "Whatever the mind can conceive and believe, it can achieve." Well, that is only a half-truth. Do you know anyone who came up with an idea, then believed and invested in it, only to have it fail? I do. That was me. That's why I was in a trade high school hitting my fingers with a hammer instead of hitting the nail on the head.

I submit to you that you are future-present, because at some point you will hear a conversation in your spirit about who you are becoming. As a spiritual being, what you hear expands your lexicology (the study of how words are structured and stored in your mental lexicon), and the neural mechanism in the brain that controls comprehension and production begins to program your tongue to say what you hear and see. So the question becomes: Did you hear your future first, or did you see it? I submit to you a new way of thinking. You heard about your future in your spirit first and then began to repeat verbally what you heard. Then you started acting "as if" your future was happening in the present.

When you *Shift Your Brilliance*, you flip the script. Simply put, when everyone and everything is figuratively screaming gloom and doom, don't buy into the hype. Walk the other way and take control of your inner steering wheel.

You finally realize that life is not a remote control, but you *can* change the channel on your tell-a-vision. This is the essence of *Shift Your Brilliance* in a nutshell. That's your *Vujá dé Moment,* when you realize that you are creating your future every day in every way.

Here are a few tweetable mental bumper stickers for you to ponder as you SHIFT…

In Life…

When people shift their brilliance, they let go of what's not working and embrace what will work.

When you shift your brilliance, you move from seeking success to finding significance.

When you shift your brilliance, you stop pushing your way into the future and begin to pull the future toward you.

When you shift your brilliance, you become the missing piece to the puzzle of the right situation.

When you shift your brilliance, you bless and release what is no longer relevant to your destiny.

When you shift your brilliance, you wake up to the fact that you are not damaged goods, but sometimes you can be in a damaging situation.

When you shift your brilliance, you realize that the future is for sale, and you buy it when you decide to own the moment.

When you shift your brilliance, in the words of my mentee Christine Bowen, you become the "total package"—wired to be brilliant.

When you shift your brilliance, you understand that money is energy. Anxiety, stress, and worry zap your energy and cut off your money flow.

In Work and Business...

When you shift your brilliance, you stop working a job and start going the extra mile without being told to do so.

When you shift your brilliance, you stop selling and start connecting. When you sell, that's a transaction, but when you connect, you build a meaningful relationship.

Let me give you an example. Peter Bond managed Dunnhumby's engagement with Coca-Cola. He accumulated over 20 different custom iPhone covers, all with Coca-Cola brands. Whenever he was in Atlanta, Georgia (Coke's World Headquarters) for meetings, he'd swap out the cover based upon the brand or group with whom he was meeting. When he sat down and casually placed his iPhone on the table, it always sparked a conversation that led to an opportunity to share his passion for their brand. This built trust and stimulated a desire to share information that led to business opportunities.

One day he was meeting with the President of the Minute Maid division and noticed that the president had a ratty old iPhone cover. Peter decided to custom design an iPhone cover with the Minute Maid logo and the message "powered by Dunnhumby" in small print at the bottom. A week after mailing the cover to him, Peter received a hand-written note thanking him for the unexpected gift. The president said that his kids now think he's cool and everyone asks where he got this unique accessory. He also insisted that Peter meet with him each time he visits Houston, and countless people at Coca-Cola have approached Peter after the president shared with them the story.

Peter told me that it may have been a "salesy" technique, but it opened many doors. He found a way to go the extra mile.

When you shift your brilliance, you become a leader with a vision instead of a boss with an agenda.

When you shift your brilliance, customer service evolves into customer love.

When you shift your brilliance, you become what author and thought leader Seth Godin calls the linchpin in business.

When you shift your brilliance, you solve problems, find solutions, and lead without a title.

When you shift your brilliance, your business moves from performance reviews to career investment discussions.

When you shift your brilliance, you live the brand of your company from the inside out and create brilliant experiences for everyone you serve.

When you shift your brilliance, you start to show up and actually "care" about being productive.

When you shift your brilliance, you realize that in the future you will be paid for the value you create and the difference you make.

When I reflect back on my formative years of growing up in Buffalo, New York, I now realize that everything that I experienced—good, bad, or indifferent—was a piece in my life's puzzle. When you embrace the pieces of your life's puzzle, you no longer force fit your way into any situation. You relax and live from the inside out.

Here are a few characteristics of individuals who shifted their brilliance:

They exude positive energy in the midst of negativity.

Happiness is their calling card.

People either like them or not.

They attract attention in a crowded room without saying a word.

They're highly intuitive—always dialed into what is happening in the world.

They operate with tacit knowledge; that is, they don't know how they do what they do; they just do it with confidence. There is no app that you can download to gain this type of edge.

Something shifts inside of you when you are in their presence.

They are agents of change. They are not afraid of change; they create it. If they are on the receiving end of change, they embrace it.

They repel inferior energy.

They may be alone but never lonely.

Worry is foreign to them because in the quantum field of life, they understand how to de-emotionalize themselves by keeping a cool head when drama surrounds them.

Men and women who shift intentionally feed their spirit unlimited possibilities. They operate with the knowledge that every possibility carries within it what thought leader Tony Miller calls, "the power of fulfillment."

Okay, let me land the plane. Harvey Mackay, author of *The Mackay MBA of Selling in the Real World*, shares a powerful insight about the Japanese Koi fish, which has unlimited growth potential. When the Koi fish is put into a small fish bowl, it will only grow two or three inches in length. But when it is put into a larger tank or even small pond, it will grow six to ten inches. If placed in an even bigger pond, it will grow to one and one half feet. Finally, if it is put into a large lake where it can really stretch out, it will grow to three feet. The size of the fish is proportional to the size of its environment.

Individuals and businesses that shift understand that the size of their future is only limited by the size of their quantum field. When you shift, you invite the world to mirror back to you what you are releasing into the atmosphere. You, as a spirit being, grow in direct proportion to the size of the environment in which you choose to live. Why conform? Be audacious.

WHY SHIFT & WHY NOW?

Shift Your Brilliance

The phrases "shift your brilliance" and "vujá dé" will be used somewhat interchangeably throughout this book, but each plays a slightly different role in the production of your life. To give credit where credit is due, it was actually the late comedian George Carlin who coined the phrase "Vujá dé" (pronounced voo-ja day). To him it meant the opposite of déjà vu, which according to Dictionary. com is "the illusion of having previously experienced something actually being encountered for the first time," or "disagreeable familiarity or sameness." A Vujá dé moment is when you see everything as if for the first time, or better still, you see everything everyone else sees, but you understand it differently, more keenly. So what does it mean to shift your brilliance? The "shift" is simply putting to action the awareness that you need to focus your energy in new, different directions—it's that inner signal of change on the horizon and having the capacity to facilitate that change through your brilliant ideas, unique contributions, and futuristic thinking.

My Personal Shift Story

I have a confession to make. It was getting pretty easy for me to dispense advice—to put my finger on the pulse of the marketplace and make declarations about problems and solutions. And it has always been second nature for me to encourage other people to live meaningful lives and to become their most brilliant selves.

Since leaving my job as Sales Director of Disney Institute at the Happiest Place on Earth—Walt Disney World—to launch the Brilliance Institute, Inc., I had been on a roll. In less than seven years, *Meetings and Conventions* magazine had cited me as one of the top keynote speakers ever heard or used. This put me in the same category with Bill Gates, Colin Powell, and Tony Robbins.

The Society of Human Resource Management asked me to be a backup speaker to Lance Armstrong in case his private plane didn't make it to Las Vegas in time for the opening general session; the society just mentioned in passing that it would have 15,000 leaders from 70 countries. I didn't even break a sweat. I said to myself, "Bring it on, Baby." Well, as fate would have it, he did show up, but it was sure nice to be wanted (even as a backup).

After 13 rejection letters from major book publishers, I had also finally sold the rights to my book *Release Your Brilliance* to Harper-Collins, and they published it in hardcover. It went on to become seventeenth out of the top 100 books being read by Corporate America, according to 800-CEO-READ. Currently it is available in English, Spanish, and Portuguese and will soon be available in other languages.

After seven magical years and four different jobs at Disney and then my own consulting business with 300 different organizations from Fortune 500 companies, educational institutions, and government agencies in less than eight years, I realized I'd learned some valuable lessons and enjoyed some great success.

What I didn't realize at the time, though, was that my work was suddenly becoming mechanical, as if I were running on cruise control. In fact, I realize now that my heart was yearning for something else. It was trying to get me to go in a different direction. But business was good, and my head and my hands kept me doing the same things I'd been doing. They suspended me in a comfort zone; they refused to stretch beyond it.

The truth is that I was holding on to what had worked yesterday, thinking it would carry me into tomorrow. I was driving a Delta 88 in a Telsa world. But as fate would have it, something intervened—something interrupted my pleasant reverie and shook me to my very core.

It was around the time Barack Obama was elected President of the United States, and our already reeling economy was getting even worse. I looked with horror at my future bookings for speaking engagements and saw that for a solid 30-day period, there were none. The calendar was empty! And there were only drips of business in the coming months.

How could this be happening? The truth was hard to accept: My business was surviving on life support, holding on by a thread, and for the first time in my career, I felt a surge of panic. Up until that moment, everything I had done had worked for me. Suddenly, I went from confidence—bolstering and cheering on others—to feeling anything but optimistic. I, who had always rebuked and flagrantly dared pessimism to come my way, felt suddenly and severely dejected.

Finding myself in this state, I turned instinctively to prayer and time on the sideline to search for answers. I crossed and uncrossed my fingers a lot. I found myself opening and shutting the refrigerator door even more. Yet it wasn't food I was hungry for. My stomach wasn't what was empty; it was my soul. I was literally stuck in neutral, going nowhere fast. I knew I needed a major shift in my thinking and doing. How could I inspire brilliance in others if I lacked that clarity and passion for myself?

About that time, I connected with a client who was planning to host a business meeting for Merck-Serono Pharmaceuticals in Paris. They booked me to speak at the conference and I accepted. The presentation topic was "How to Release Your Brilliance."

As I packed for the trip and made the journey across the Atlantic, I realized it had been ten years since I had last been to Paris. It was on that previous trip, at age 30 and with Disney, while standing underneath the Eiffel Tower that I had reflected on the words of Dick Nunis (former chairman of Walt Disney Attractions). He said, "The higher you go, the less you know." I realized in that instant that I had gone as far as I could go at Disney, even though at one time I had said I wanted to be the Chairman and CEO one day.

I decided to do the unthinkable—leave my wonderful job at Walt Disney World and start my own consulting and speaking business. As good as the Disney organization had been for and to me, I realized that it was time to move on to the next stage in my life. It was my Vujá dé Moment.

Something about that sky-piercing, elegant Parisian architectural icon had vitalized me. It was a profound moment. Something truly monumental happened to me that day, and I knew I'd never be the same. I decided to ascend the staircase of the Eiffel Tower instead of taking the elevator lift. The higher I went, the more challenging it became. It was in this moment that I realized I was climbing the stairs because I knew in my heart that I belonged at the top of anything and everything I did. It was as if there were an internal click, a voice directing me to move, and I had finally discovered my purpose. For a brief moment I saw into my own crystal ball of choice.

When I returned home, my wife and I discussed what my next move would be. I'll never forget what she said: "No matter what, I am with you." Wow! That was the vote of confidence I needed. It was what gave me the courage to turn down four job offers in a 90-day period—offers that would have been easier to take rather than risking it all to follow my heart and what seemed like a calling.

My wife's unwavering dedication, my strong faith, and the memory of the elegant and inspiring tower created the momentum that allowed me to shift and set off into the unknown. There were no guarantees and no backup plan. This had to work.

Now a decade later, it was with both excitement and a bit of apprehension that I set out for my second trip to the City of Light. I had a feeling that, once again, things weren't going to be the same when I returned.

As I walked along the Champs-Elysees and into the nearby neighborhoods, the first thing I noticed was what a difference time makes. I'd endured a lot of change, both good and bad. My hair had grayed a bit, and I had begun to see my friends and family members pass away, reminding me just how precious life is. I no longer fought to hold back tears, now comfortable with my emotions in a way I hadn't been ten years earlier. It had taken me 40 years to get to this point, but I realized that I was free—liberated from the limitations of my past, from living a life just to please other people, and free to believe in and choose my own values. Free to *Vujá dé*—to live my future now.

Standing before the Eiffel Tower once again, I listened for the voice I had so distinctly heard ten years before, and to my astonishment, I believe I really did hear something. It was a small but insistent voice, and it was repeating the same message I'd been receiving both in my heart and head for the past 18 months.

This time, the voice was very clear. It was telling me to *shift*.

I knew I had to get involved in my work in a deeper way. I had to make a deeper commitment. I knew that when I returned to the States, I needed to pour more into my writing; make it more substantive, direct, crisp. I needed to reveal my truths more honestly. I wanted to forge more profound, authentic connections with my clients and readers.

After several months of staying true to this new goal, I can honestly say it has made a huge difference in my life and my work. While I was already receiving positive responses to my monthly e-newsletter that goes out to thousands of people, it was little compared to now. People used to tell me that my words had inspired them, but nothing like they are telling me now.

My personal shift has taught me to be laser-focused. I'm no longer driving in circles or in many directions all at once. As a direct result of my shifting, my consulting company has grown and impacted a greater number of clients and a wider reading audience. I'm proud to say that (along with my amazing team, because I never could have done it without them) the National Speakers Association selected me as one of the top 25 "hot speakers" shaping the profession. Furthermore, while I was writing this book, Nido Qubein, author and speaker extraordinaire and president of High Point University, nominated me to the Speaker Hall of Fame for platform excellence.

By finding my courage and support in others, looking at things in a new way, and crystallizing a vision to take me to new levels of meaning and success, I was able to ignite my passion and shift. Here are some questions to consider:

- What could a personal shift do for you?

- Are you holding on to what worked yesterday?

- Are you suppressing your inner voice that is telling you to step out of your comfort zone?

- What mysterious voice or vision are you ignoring?

- Can you immerse yourself in your work or in your relationships in a more significant way?

Read this book as the first step to finding the power and inspiration to SHIFT! While *Vujá dé* is the what, *shifting your brilliance* is the how.

Brilliant Shifts All Around Us

My mentor and friend, Dan Burrus, takes a different spin on Vujá dé in his book *Flash Foresight*. According to him:

> …it is a blinding flash of the future obvious. It is an intuitive grasp of the foreseeable future that, once you see it, reveals hidden opportunities and allows you to solve your biggest problems—before they happen. Flash Foresight will allow anyone to both see and shape his or her future.

Bill Taylor, co-founder of *Fast Company* magazine, says in his book *Practically Radical*,

> Vujá dé is looking at a familiar situation (an industry you've worked in for decades, products you've worked on for years) as if you've never seen it before, and, with that fresh line of sight, developing a distinctive point of view on the future…vujá dé may be a strange term, but it's become a strangely popular term among some of the brightest thinkers on creativity.

Vujá dé is a twist on conventional wisdom.

Jean-Marie Dru, author of *Disruption: Overturning Conventions and Shaking up the Marketplace,* says, "It is a matter of questioning the way things are, of breaking with what has been done or seen before, of rejecting the conventional."

A modern-day example of a business that employs a shift of brilliance thinking is a relatively new company called Uber. With the creation of its downloadable apps, Uber is "evolving the way the world moves," through connecting taxi and private car riders with drivers at the touch of a button. The company has launched in over 35 cities and has globally disrupted the taxi and private car space, and in turn, has shifted how we arrange transportation. CEO and Co-Founder, Travis Kalanick, states on the website, "Every problem has a solution. You just have to be creative enough to find it." Only this kind of shift in brilliance can propel a company from a niche market in one city to a global presence less than five years later.

Cirque du Soleil is another example. If you've been to one of their performances, you know it's the circus on steroids— prescribed ones. Using a fresh set of eyes, they shifted what we normally thought of as a circus in a profound way. Most people feel that a Ringling Bros. and Barnum & Bailey circus performance is no comparison to one of Cirque du Soleil's. (Of course, the ticket price is about seven times that of Ringling Bros.) How many times do people leave a regular circus show and rave about how great it was? Very rarely, I bet. Why? There is no shift of brilliance.

There are many ways to shift your brilliance. Start by looking for the uncommon in the common, for the meaning behind the actions and the words, for the new in the old. Like the entrepreneurs at Uber and Cirque du Soleil, you too, can discover innovative and breakthrough solutions. And, I promise you don't have to have really cool apps or a flying trapeze.

Why Vujá dé?

My friend, Israel Houghton, a four-time Grammy award-winning artist, said during a live recording, "Life doesn't happen when the alarm goes off. It happens when you wake up." That's the Vujá dé Moment in a nutshell, making the Shift from Average to Brilliant. It's when you wake up from the deep hibernation of average living and of waiting for things to change for the better to exceptional living and generating change. It's what the folks at Microsoft taught me—"What are we going to Go-Do?"

To me, a Vujá dé Moment is a feeling of confidence about what lies ahead. Now, I'm not suggesting some kind of eerie magic or fortune telling. I'm talking about the uncanny, not the occult. Déjà vu and Vujá dé are both about sensation—a compelling sense of familiarity with something unseen. But Vujá dé is about the future. It is about envisioning and believing in the possibilities—believing in the future so strongly that those possibilities become proverbial, as if they are real. Vujá dé is seeing—and living—your future as if it's happening now.

Vujá dé is all about shifting. It's when you have confirmation in your gut about making important changes without having to have external validation. It's the ability to see and believe in your own potential and the potential of the team around you. Vujá dé is realizing that there will come a time when you will have to break with the old to embrace the new, to let go of what is comfortable and convenient in order to grow and expand.

It's about moving in a new direction without a map, GPS, or support from your Facebook friends. It's doing the exact opposite of what you've always done in order to ignite a creative spark of new possibility. Because it's a promise of greater things ahead, Vujá dé is the moment when everything clicks and you decide to resist the gravitational pull that keeps you from being brilliant.

Vujá dé is the big idea. It's the breakthrough. It's the disruption from your normal routine. If you intend to live brilliantly, then accept that disruption is your future. In fact, look at your calendar; disruption is your next appointment. So, why Vuja dé? I believe our lives and destinies beckon us to these Vuja dé moments, because they become our exercise machines of hope, and ultimately, this hope is what propels us forward to accomplish great things.

Why Shift Your Brilliance?

So, why is it so important to shift your brilliance, and why now? Let's look at what it means to shift.

To shift is to move from one place, position, or direction to another. As a term, the earliest usage for "shift" meant seismic activity. An earthquake, also known as a tremor, is the result of a sudden release of energy. These seismic events—whether natural phenomena or caused by humans—generate waves. At the earth's surface, quakes manifest themselves by shifting and displacing the ground.

Maybe you are experiencing a similar phenomenon. Perhaps you are feeling the sensation of pent-up energy, a bubbling surge of inner power, and an uncontrollable urge to release it. You may know it's time to make a change—to create some waves of your own, so to speak. Whether in your personal or professional life, you may be feeling a pull or the need to displace one aspect of your life with another. You're sensing the signs of a sudden but powerful rupture, or at least a disruption from your normal routine.

When you shift it leads to new discoveries…if you are open, present, and willing to pause and analyze what's really going on and reflect on what you can learn from it. For individuals, shifts present an opportunity to refocus on what matters most, to de-clutter your heart, mind, and soul, and to uncover hidden seeds of brilliance within you.

For businesses, disruptive shifts offer the chance to modify your products and/or services to better align with current trends or to develop inventive, alternative products or services. Shifting your business in response to, or anticipation of, consumer demand ensures your organization will stay relevant and profitable in an every-changing economy.

If you are doing things the way you have always done them, then invite disruption in. You do not have the luxury of maintaining a wait-and-see attitude. That is a slow-moving strategy that leads to becoming obsolete.

We're going through a time of uncertainty; we're on shaky ground; we're all feeling the tremors of an unstable economy and government shutdown. Or maybe things for you are okay the way they are; or at least your life is stable. But ask yourself, "Is okay good enough?" Will a shift in your brilliance offer you something else out there that maybe seems out of reach but holds the promise of a better future? What if you were to submit to your hunch that this inner energy might create new opportunities? What if you could conjure up the courage to break through the surface of your current situation? Could the reward for deciding to shift your life and business outweigh the risk? My bet is YES!

David Houle, in his brilliant book *The Shift Age*, states:

> We live in the Shift Age, a time of transformation that will
> be regarded by future historians as one of the most signif-
> icant periods in human history. How we navigate the first
> 25 years of this millennium will determine whether these
> future historians praise our perspicacity or wonder why

we failed to grasp the evolutionary imperatives so obvious to them.

The reality is everything around us and everything we once knew has shifted. Our once-trusted retirement funds have been weakened significantly. The health of our financial system is not as robust as we were all led to believe. We trusted that our homes were our greatest assets, but the mortgage industry has sagged and now for-sale signs are yellowing in front yards everywhere. Foreign currency flows between and through countries, and companies are no longer restricted to the countries in which they operate. CEOs want talent—people who possess a creative spark and an innovative bent that will enable their companies to extend their brands.

Changes and global shifts are taking place all the time. These dynamics impact cultures, products, systems, and the way we make decisions on a daily basis—as businesses and as individuals. More often than not, these shifts require us to change our mindsets in order to cope, or, simply put, Vujá dé everything we do…as well as adopt the seven steps described in this book to deliberately shift ourselves into the future.

That's exactly what HR Manager Heidi McConnell did after hearing me speak at a business conference. She wrote,

> I was feeling stuck, overwhelmed and uninspired by all of my projects at hand. I didn't know where to start or prioritize. I wanted to throw in the towel and say "I can't do it." Instead, I put everything aside and started working on some simple daily tasks, and it hit me. I needed to shift my thinking. I could do this; I do know how to do it or can learn. I started small, first prioritizing by due dates, then I created simple outlines and steps for each project. Before I knew it I had everything I needed to complete

these projects and was successful. By stepping away, taking a breather, and changing my attitude, I was able to see the light, and that's how I owned my moment!

Examples of shifts in brilliance are all around us. Nick Coleman, General Manager of a well-known designer spa chain, released his brilliance with staff members while away at a conference. Whenever they called him with a question, problem, or concern, he resisted the urge to immediately solve the problem for them and instead asked them probing questions, which ultimately led them to the answers. Though this took more time and patience, he realized that he was empowering his team and building confidence by leading them to their own solutions. This helped boost his staff's ability to make the right decisions and taught them to trust their instincts in problem solving. In reflecting on his shift, Nick says, "I am always there for them, regardless, but now I can share the responsibilities and we can all feel a little more brilliant!"

Entrepreneur and business owner, Emily Shelton, shifted her brilliance when she set out on a quest to answer a question posed at one of my seminars: "Does what you want, want you?" She decided to create a simple three-column spreadsheet that would help her visually answer this question. Column one had the header: What I want; column two's header read: What I'm doing to get it; and column three was headed: How I know it wants me back. Simple, but powerful! She used this spreadsheet to document her goals, action items, and results, giving her a very tangible tool of accountability. I predict this type of shift in thinking will lead to brilliant outcomes.

Another major way I encourage you to shift your brilliance is to continually push yourself beyond your comfort zone. Ethan Goldman, a corporate director, wrote to me that he has started assembling his "personal board of directors." He reached out to three senior executives in his company that he felt he could learn from and whom he knew would be willing and able to provide him with candid feedback. One of them he would be working closely with, as he had agreed to assume the role of chair for an internal Leadership Group, and the other two he had requested to be a part of large projects for which they were going to be assembling teams. They agreed to include him. He felt as if this would be an opportunity for him to network outside his comfort zone and to challenge and stretch his current abilities, plus give him more visibility with these respected leaders.

For more examples and exercises on how you can adopt this mindset, visit www.shiftyourbrilliance.com.

History offers countless examples of shifting into brilliance and Vujá dé that have served to break apart seemingly stable industries and put them back together in a completely different way. To the surprise of some, there will still be a mandate for Vujá dé thinking to continue no matter how successful you are as a company or how long you've been around. This is a lesson I learned well from my former employer, The Walt Disney Company.

Despite being "the" standard for excellence in all things family entertainment, I was always amazed at the company's insistence to "never rest on its laurels" (in the words of Walt Disney himself). New products, merchandise, attractions, and offerings continued to be introduced year after year, always surpassing the expectations of consumers and guests.

Similarly, one would think a company like NASA with an inception dating back to the late 1950s and basically no industry competitor would be able to rest easy on past accomplishments. Not in the least.

Not only has NASA not rested, contrarily the organization continues to take missions and programs to new heights, ensuring the

United States will remain the world's leader in space exploration and scientific discovery for years to come. For future exploration, NASA is yet again reinventing itself and designing and building the capabilities to send humans to explore the solar system, working toward a goal of sending humans to a captured, relocated asteroid in the next decade and even landing humans on Mars by the 2030s. Wow…talk about not resting on your laurels and shifting your brilliance!

Those who thought Vujá dé was a passing fad woke up one day to find that their marketplace had disappeared. Don't let that be you! You are probably saying, "Simon, what should I do?" My friend, it's very simple: Disrupt thyself! Intentionally reinvent. Be curious about everything. Ask profound questions. Go the opposite direction. Unleash the inner salmon. Flip the script.

There are many other companies that have intentionally shifted their brilliance and explored their own versions of Vujá dé to remain in the forefront. Here are a few examples:

- World-renowned video game maker Nintendo was established in Japan in 1889 as a maker of handmade playing cards.

- Gucci, famous for top-quality shoes and handbags, started as a small leather-goods company making everything from saddles to luggage.

- Virgin Airways is now taking reservations for people to travel into outer space and the depths of the oceans.

All of these companies were flexible, nimble, and insightful enough to proactively upset the norm and move in a new, fresh direction.

What about you? When the next disruption takes place, which side of the fence will you be on? Will you be the one initiating the disturbance or the one sitting on the other side watching it happen?

When you consider the personal impact of disruption, what comes to mind? What are you going to have to break or split from in order to soar? What bold moves do you need to make in order to live your life by design rather than by default? How can you initiate a disruption?

Simon T. Says... Shifting your brilliance is turning loose your inner salmon to swim upstream against the current of popular opinion.

Nika Stewart is a quirky, edgy, award-winning interior designer who realized after having her daughter that she needed to run her business differently. She didn't want to stop working, but she also didn't want to leave Ellie in full-time day care. Out of desperation, Nika figured out a way to use her knowledge to create a business—LaptopMom.com. The purpose was to show moms how to leverage their time, create passive income, and build successful businesses... during naptime! These mom-preneurs are shifting and having a blast.

These are just a few examples of the shifting going on around us. People like you who have been stuck in their thinking or stuck in their jobs are now shifting to make the familiar fresh.

Are you ready to Vujá dé and make a brilliant shift?

My good friend and fellow thought leader and author, Rebel Brown, was not thinking that a brilliant shift was needed in her life, but circumstances and fate led her to shift her brilliance anyway. She detailed her journey in a testimonial recently sent to me. Here is her story.

The Shifter

I wasn't looking for a shift. My life was outstanding. Business was great, I was in love, I'd just published my "change your thinking business book," *Defy Gravity*. I was already diving deeper into the human mind for another book. I just had to understand why we humans get stuck doing things the way we've always done them, even when it's not the rational choice. I'd seen it time and again in my consulting and turnaround clients. What is up with us humans?

Then the roller coaster cranked up. My love turned out to be a sociopath who loved many women at the same time. A month later I was diagnosed with Post Traumatic Stress Disorder (PTSD), something we assumed I'd created while caretaking my mom, dad, and then a friend with AIDS for some 8 years. In treatment, I recalled memories of childhood trauma I'd blocked for nearly 45 years. The day the memories came up, I began to sink into a black pit of complete powerlessness, unworthiness and defeat. I could barely get out of the house to go to my hypnotherapy sessions. For three years. I did every therapy known to man. Nothing helped. In fact, therapy only made me more powerless.

I'd shifted all right. I was curled up in a ball on the kitchen floor. Knowing I'd never be able to get up again.

Then, three years into my shift I found neuroscience, the study of the human mind. My curiosity spiked, and I began to dive in deep. What I learned about the technology of our minds and what makes us humans tick changed my life forever.

It will change yours too. Why care about the technology of your mind? We all think we're logical rational beings. Neuroscience is learning that we're really not. In fact, our unconscious mind drives 90% of our thinking, behaviors, and decisions. Our conscious mind never gets involved. Read that again and think about it.

"Wait a minute. I think and decide all the time. Way more than 10% of the time..."

Actually, we don't. We just think we do, based on the information our conscious mind receives. But here's what really happens.

We take in 11,000,000 bits/second of data through our senses.

Our unconscious mind filters that data, deciding what is relevant and important to pass onto our conscious mind.

Our unconscious uses mindware* programs from our past (memories, decisions, values, emotions and more) as well as our expectations and focus at any point in time to select the data it shares with our conscious mind.

Only 126 bits of that 11,000,000 bits/second is sent to our conscious selves. That's right—we only consciously recognize 126 bits out of the vast data we take in. Talk about selective perception!

Just think how many other realities, how many diverse points of data are in the 10,999,874 bits/second that our conscious mind never receives. Now think about all the unconscious programs that are literally deciding your specific reality, right now.

Imagine taking control of those unconscious programs to shift your reality to be what you really want. Imagine being able to release the limiting beliefs and decisions, programmed throughout your life experience, to step into your full brilliance and power?

You can. Thanks to the technology of your mind. If you change your mind, you'll change your world. Once I really understood how my mind was working for me, I was able to literally shift the mindware programs that held me as being powerless.

Using a technique I call Quantum Mind Mechanics, I changed my programming; from powerless to powerful, from unworthy to abundant, from defeated to limitless. We can all do the same shifting. It's simple, painless and takes minutes to a few hours. The shift is nothing short of transformational.

As we focus on our problem, we reinforce and expand the mindware program that reinforces that problem in our lives. The more we focus, the more power that problem has over our lives. That's how our minds works. Whatever we focus on and expect is what our unconscious mind thinks we want. So it creates a program to deliver just that to us. Focus on the problem, and you get more of the problem.

The transformation of my own mind was the best gift ever. Within three hours, all of my childhood horror and the mindware programs associated with it were released. After another two hours, all the other limiting beliefs and negative emotions, developed as a result of my childhood, were also released.

I was able to look at all the sad memories, hear all the scary voices and feel all of the sadness and powerlessness as an objective observer. I still remember wondering, "How the heck could I ever have believed that?" as I thought about my state of mind just the day before. For the first time in my life, I was free of the scary voices that drove me for over four decades.

My results were so powerful. I decided to focus on this technology in my career, applying the power of our minds to business and professional success. The amazing technology of our minds isn't just for our personal selves, or clearing bad memories or other human conditions. This technology has the power to transform our businesses and our professional worlds.

We are humans in business. Our unconscious minds drive our thinking, behaviors and decisions in our business and personal worlds. By applying the technology of our minds to our business pursuits, we can and will influence the next generation of human performance to create breakout business results.

Imagine:

- Getting inside the mind of your customers to understand how and why they make the decisions they make. Then using that information to present your proposal in a way that exactly matches how they think about and process their decisions.

- Influencing individuals, teams and entire organizations by leading their unconscious minds; communicating in the best manner for each individual, matching individuals to their best roles, motivating each and every team member to their best performance ever. That's only the beginning.

- Now imagine stepping beyond the limiting beliefs about yourself, your business, your market and your products. Imagine stepping into a limitless world filled with innovation, action and results.

That's the power of the technology of your mind applied to your business and professional self. From breakout strategies to influential leadership, from expanded new business to dramatically accelerated and increased revenues— when you apply neuroscience to your business, the results will follow.

Today, I have shifted my brilliance, and I'm more passionate than ever about my own life, about the life-changing work I do every day with people, and about the technology of our minds. I now know our minds are capable of stepping into the next generation of human performance. I'm blessed to guide people to do just that every single day.

Why I Wrote This Book

I wrote this book for people like Rebel and you; to inspire you to tune into your own little hints to shift your brilliance; to encourage you to listen to your own inner voice—a voice perhaps too long silenced by fear and apprehension; and to hearten you to watch for glimpses of what your future holds and what you can become.

I wrote it in the hope that you will shift your prospective achievements to the present.

Good enough has become the enemy of great.
Routine has become the enemy of desire.
Easy has become the enemy of sacrifice and hard work!
—Kevin and Jackie Freiberg, authors of *BOOM.*

Many people tend to rely on cruise control, traveling along at one speed. Although this may provide for a more relaxing and safe ride at times, too much time in cruise control can actually present a risk. It can put your mind in a state that impairs your ability to react to bumps in the road or unexpected needs to veer or merge.

Shifting moves you away from cruising and puts you back in control of your journey.

It is my hope that the messages and tools in this book fire you up and motivate you to make necessary shifts in your own life, just as I was forced to do in my own. (And just think how much money I will have saved you because you won't have to travel all the way to Paris for that inspiration!)

I wrote this book to help you shift into drive and accelerate toward your destination of personal success, regardless of the road you are on now.

Every day most of us shift the gears in our vehicles. We move the gearshift from park to reverse, from reverse to drive and, depending on the car, we shift through the gears as we accelerate. Sometimes we are intentional when we shift; other times it is subconscious.

The truth is, we are natural shifters. Human beings are *meant* to shift. We shift from grade school to high school, from dependency to self-sufficiency, from job to job, from being single to being married, and from childhood to adulthood and often, parenthood. Our entire lives are about shifting—toward our destination.

But sometimes we get stuck in neutral and we need that jump-start to get us moving again. This book is your tool and inspiration to get you moving, to propel you, to make you be more deliberate about your choice and intentional about your future.

You now hold in your hand a personal invitation to SHIFT your brilliance!

Vision Check: Do You Need to *Shift?*

Maybe you're on the verge of moving forward, or maybe you're suspended in the present and need a push and a plan to turn the key. Maybe you've been asking yourself the same question that I asked: *How do I know if I need to shift?* Here's a twenty-seven question reality check. Respond to these questions to assess your need to shift.

STEP 1: See Differently						
1 = to no extent 2 = to a small extent 3 = to some extent 4 = to a considerable extent 5 = to a great extent						
1.	I consistently try to do things differently.	1	2	3	4	5
2.	I willingly step outside my comfort zone.	1	2	3	4	5
3.	I have a clear picture in my mind about what my future looks like.	1	2	3	4	5
SUBTOTAL YOUR ANSWERS #1-3:						

STEP 2: Harness The Power of You, Inc.						
1 = to no extent 2 = to a small extent 3 = to some extent 4 = to a considerable extent 5 = to a great extent						
4.	I am confident about my ability to create the future.	1	2	3	4	5
5.	I think of new ways to solve old problems.	1	2	3	4	5
6.	I seek ways to bring value to any environment I am in.	1	2	3	4	5
SUBTOTAL YOUR ANSWERS #4-6:						

STEP 3: Ignite A Fresh Vision
1 = to no extent 2 = to a small extent 3 = to some extent
4 = to a considerable extent 5 = to a great extent

7.	I take advantage of every opportunity that presents itself.	1	2	3	4	5
8.	I always look for ways to support my team members.	1	2	3	4	5
9.	I take ownership in any situation to ensure that the business thrives.	1	2	3	4	5

SUBTOTAL YOUR ANSWERS #7-9:

STEP 4: Fuel Your Mind
1 = to no extent 2 = to a small extent 3 = to some extent
4 = to a considerable extent 5 = to a great extent

10.	I use the tools that I need to stay relevant in any economy.	1	2	3	4	5
11.	I reframe failure as a learning opportunity.	1	2	3	4	5
12.	I enjoy learning from my team members.	1	2	3	4	5

SUBTOTAL YOUR ANSWERS #10-12:

13.	I project a positive, healthy, and realistic self-image in every situation.	1	2	3	4	5
14.	I have the coping skills to make the best of any situation.	1	2	3	4	5
15.	I study my customer's business and industry.	1	2	3	4	5

SUBTOTAL YOUR ANSWERS #13-15:

16.	I am passionate about my work.	1	2	3	4	5
17.	I am seen as a subject matter expert by peers.	1	2	3	4	5
18.	I am accountable for growing and producing results.	1	2	3	4	5

SUBTOTAL YOUR ANSWERS #16-18:

STEP 5: Take the Wheel
1 = to no extent 2 = to a small extent 3 = to some extent
4 = to a considerable extent 5 = to a great extent

19.	I have balance in my life.	1	2	3	4	5
20.	I welcome directions and feedback that help me produce better results.	1	2	3	4	5
21.	I operate in self-awareness and make necessary changes to move forward.	1	2	3	4	5

SUBTOTAL YOUR ANSWERS #19-21:

STEP 6: Engage Your Gears
1 = to no extent 2 = to a small extent 3 = to some extent
4 = to a considerable extent 5 = to a great extent

22.	I adapt new habits to create the best outcomes.	1	2	3	4	5
23.	I believe in creating memorable moments for the customer.	1	2	3	4	5
24.	I know how to deliver value and results in life and business.	1	2	3	4	5

SUBTOTAL YOUR ANSWERS #22-24:

STEP 7: Restart Your Engine
1 = to no extent 2 = to a small extent 3 = to some extent
4 = to a considerable extent 5 = to a great extent

25.	I know what I need to do to stay engaged to produce meaningful work that matters.	1	2	3	4	5
26.	I anticipate the needs of my customers before they ask for help.	1	2	3	4	5
27.	I own the moment and choose to make something happen.	1	2	3	4	5

SUBTOTAL YOUR ANSWERS #25-27:

TOTAL

Thank you for completing the Shift Your Brilliance Assessment. Visit www.shiftyourbrilliance.com to connect to the community, share your story, and sustain your brilliance.

Add up your scores:

100-135: Congratulations, O Brilliant One! You are a shifter and in control of your destiny. Read on to discover how to maintain your momentum. Also, download a free App from www.shiftyourbrilliance.com.

64-99: You see the possibilities and most likely know it's time to shift. Make sure that you complete the exercises in the book and sign up for the 12 week Shift to Brilliance Course at www.shiftyourbrilliance.com.

29-63: You are stuck in neutral and need a jumpstart to get going again. It's never too late, though! Read the entire book with an account-ability partner, and sign up for the 12 week Shift to Brilliance and actively participate in the Shift Your Brilliance community—www.shiftyourbrilliance.com, and find the power to get Harness the Power of You, Inc.

SHIFTER: Your Guide to Action

So what do you do? How do you take control of your life and become a shifter? How do you make sure that rather than being shifted, manipulated by others or the environment, you are the one behind the wheel with your clutch within reach? Yes, we're living in an era where we're witnessing seismic shifts of enormous proportions. However, individuals who shift become intentional about their lives and thus become unstoppable in creating their futures. Why?

When you decide it's time for a change, you experience a Vujá dé Moment and you shift into your brilliance. You develop an appetite for adventure in an effort to ensure a spectacular tomorrow.

In the Disney/Pixar movie *Cars,* John Lasseter tells the story of Lightning McQueen, who focuses on being the fastest car in racing instead of realizing the real reward in life is embracing all of the changes that occur along the journey. Michael Wallis, a Pulitzer Prize-nominated historian and consultant to Disney/Pixar on the movie *Cars,* says:

> Route 66 is the most famous highway in the world, and it represents the great American road trip. It's a chance to drive from Chicago, through the heartland and the Southwest, past ribbons of neon, across the great Mojave, to the Pacific shore at Santa Monica. Every road has a look based on where the road goes.

People who decide to make a shift see their life like a road trip along Route 66. They may not know what is around the next corner, but they have given themselves permission to accept and not judge it; to ask "how" instead of "what," and to allow change to move through them instead of accepting "it's just happening to them." Shifting is not about speeding up or slowing down; it's about giving yourself permission to change lanes at your own pace. It's about believing in your vision of tomorrow, today.

Vicki Arkoff provides the back-story of this popular movie in her blog. She writes that Lasseter packed his entire family into a motor home and set out on a two-month trip with the goal of staying off the interstate highways and dipping his toes into both the Pacific and Atlantic oceans. The trip brought the family closer together. "Suddenly I realized what the film needed to be about," Lasseter said. "That the journey in life is the reward. It's great to achieve things, but when you do, you want to have your family and friends around to help celebrate."

Somewhere on the Route 66 of Life, you will discover that the movie of *your* life should be called *Is This It?* I have discovered in my own journey that we have the potential to reach the place that Noel Burch, of Gordon Training International, calls "unconscious competence." This is when an individual has had so much practice with a skill that it becomes second nature, and it can be performed easily (often without concentrating too deeply). When you reach this point, then you have to ask yourself, "Is this it, or is there another level of possibility, or another dimension of expansion, a better adventure that I don't yet see or believe exists?"

Another way to think about becoming a shifter is to consider the use of the term "game changer" in the world of stocks and investments. In a recent blog, I read, "A game changer defines or redefines the sector where it competes…sets the pricing and margin model in its sector…and explores new geographies for its products, and in many cases betters mankind." As an individual, you can be a game changer instead of being changed by the game.

In this context, you might argue that a McDonald's Big Mac does not better mankind, but McDonald's has made a powerful effort to offer more healthful items on its menu. A game changer, regardless of current size, grows its revenues and earnings at the highest levels within its respective sector. Other examples of game changers are Apple, Google, and Caterpillar—and in its heyday, Saturn. (See www.bloggingstocks.com/meet-the-game-changers-companies.)

As a game changer, or shifter, you can define or redefine your life's work and universal assignment. You can raise the bar and the level of expectation at your place of business. Like these big players, you can, on a more scalable level, explore new opportunities and refuse to settle for the status quo. A game changer, regardless of current economy, limitations, or forecast, will find a way.

Game changers realize their limited time on earth is to make a profound difference in the marketplace, in their neighborhoods, in their families. They don't wait for the game to come to them. They trust their Vujá dé. They drive forward into the future with no guarantees, and along the way they will make something profound happen.

A game changer, or a shifter, understands real leadership is about leading change. Everything else is maintaining the status quo. Teams are looking for leaders who will challenge them to rise to the occasion and not forget to say thank you for a job well done. Teams increase their level of engagement when working for a leader with a vision instead of a boss with an agenda.

A shifter changes gears by deciding to leave a significant imprint instead of making a fleeting impression. Those who decide to be brilliant in whatever they set their minds to leave that kind of mark. You can see it in every field of study, every industry, every vocation. Look through the annals of history, and you will see men and women who rose to the occasion in their era and shifted the conversation. Why? They decided that mediocrity was for those who wanted to stay in neutral.

Simon T. Says... Be a game changer in your life,
industry, market, and sector. Change the game
or be forced to react to change in the game.

Vujá dé is the catalyst to your future; SHIFTING your brilliance is the tool to get you there. Follow these seven actions to get moving:

1. See differently

2. Harness the power of You, Inc.

3. Ignite a fresh vision

4. Fuel your mind

5. Take the wheel

6. Engage your gears

7. Restart your engine

The chapters of this book will take you through these seven steps of shifting to your brilliant future—complete with tips, tools, and reflection exercises that will equip you to dream, focus, and increase your potential.

Are you ready to SHIFT?

SEE DIFFERENTLY

The first step in becoming a shifter is to Vujá dé—to "see differently."

What does it mean to see differently? It means to change your mindset. When you begin to see things differently, the opportunities before you change. To shift, you must be willing to examine everything you do and ask yourself if you are creating the tomorrow you want.

> Most companies in most industries have a kind of tunnel vision. They chase the opportunities that everyone else is chasing; they miss the opportunities that everyone else is missing. It's the companies that see a different game that win big. —Bill Taylor, founder of *Fast Company* magazine

It amazes me that as human beings we become conditioned to accept what comes our way without questioning if there is a *better* way. How often do you wake up to go to work or your place of business and go through the same routine? How often do you do something the same way, at the same time, in the same place, every day?

We have a tendency to behave as creatures of habit, captive to a sameness that causes individuals and businesses alike to be stuck in neutral while the rest of the world is passing by and waving as they drive into a more hopeful future. To shift our perspective, we need to open our eyes and take a few risks. We need an inspirational Vujá dé.

I was speaking to the Society of Human Resource Management in Las Vegas and received this e-mail from a lady in attendance:

> You were the last speaker I heard, after several non-stop days filled with fantastic speakers. You challenged us to "see differently." Wow!
>
> That really, truly made an impression on me. I went up front to thank you afterward. I sputtered something about returning to Las Vegas in a few months to be a presenter at my own annual company conference and how your presentation made me realize without question that I needed to ditch my carefully crafted, and fully completed, speech and PowerPoint presentation. You graciously asked me to let you know how it all went, and you handed me your business card before I scuttled off.
>
> I've got to report my new speech and PowerPoint presentation went *phenomenally* well! I could frankly GUSH at this point. The response to my presentation was simply... staggering. I was awarded a spot on our Executive Team less than two weeks after my presentation. I'm now the ninth person in the company "at the table." Granted, I had been working very hard for some time to get to this level. Nonetheless, I just know it was my ability to

see differently, and to successfully present that different viewpoint at our national conference, that gave me the final push.

What will you do to see differently?

Most of us have either seen or heard of *Scandal*, the hugely popular and tweet-worthy ABC television drama. The show centers on a PR firm, specializing in risk management, which is made up of a close-knit team of lawyers who take unbelievable risks to "fix" the scandals of their high profile White House clientele. The team is led by the infamous "fixer," Olivia Pope, who is known for "seeing" seemingly impossible scenarios "differently." She follows her gut and finds ways to clean up public relations messes no one else would dare touch. Through tackling each problem with an unpredictable perspective, she and her team are able to strategize to survive the real or contrived scandals of the U.S. government.

This world of political conspiracy and espionage may seem worlds apart from your daily office routine. However, it is really no different for those of us who work in the corporate world. The politics and maneuvers may not look the same, but navigation still requires the gut instincts, finesse, and industry knowledge admired in Olivia Pope's character. It's an environment that can stretch you, challenge you, and force you out of your comfort zone...*if* you are an engaged "fixer" and willing to see differently to embrace the full experience. Just remember that seeing differently sometimes calls for becoming uncomfortable with being comfortable.

Try changing your mindset, try seeing your environment in a new and different light. While the problems that arise in your personal life, business, or workplace can be a mysterious and scary thing, the ability to see them through brilliant eyes and fix them like no one else can is an extraordinary, exciting, and awe-inspiring thing.

No, I won't ask you to go toe to toe with the FBI or CIA. You don't even have to be involved in any scandal whatsoever. Just open your eyes to the possibilities. See the problem in a new light, and your journey as a brilliant fixer will become a thrilling adventure that will positively impact your development…and your life.

Simon T. Says… You can survive, even thrive, through the problems that arise in your life if you change your perspective and seize opportunities.

Look Back…But Only Briefly

In order to see correctly when you drive, you need to use all of your mirrors and windows. I'm asking you to do the same to see differently. You must:

- *Look back:* Use your rearview mirror to honor the past.

- *Look sideways:* Use you side view mirrors to alter your perspective and look askance.

- *Look forward:* Use your wide-open windshield to envision the future.

There's a reason we have rearview mirrors. They lend an important perspective in our passage to brilliance. They reflect where we've been and what's following us, which influences our decisions moving forward. Who and where we are today are in large part a result of the road taken thus far. A piece of who I am today is due in part to my struggles early in life—specifically when I had to leave college for financial reasons, moved into a drug-inhabited, roach-infested neighborhood, and took a desk clerk job at the local Days Inn for $5.20 an hour. (I did return to finish my degree. It just took me ten years to complete it.)

Most of the time, to move forward we have to first shift into reverse to back out of our driveways or parking spots. We have to use our rearview mirrors. So, to shift meaningfully, it's also important to spend some time looking back. There are important discoveries to be made from delving into our pasts. Still, we don't want to dwell on what's behind us. After all, if we spend too much time looking in our rearview mirrors, we'll miss what's coming!

Dr. Barbara Fredrickson, a leading social science and positive psychology scholar based at the University of North Carolina, did a resilience study involving 100 college students. She based her survey on the work of psychology pioneer Jack Block of the University of California, Berkeley, who had gathered data over 50 years on how ordinary people fared through life's ups and downs, twists and turns. Dr. Fredrickson measured the students' psychological strengths, including their optimism, tranquility and life satisfaction. Those who scored high had flexible personality styles and bounced back faster than those who scored low. Her key finding was that these individuals possessed an uncanny resilience. To find out more about Dr. Fredrickson's brilliant insight, I suggest that you pick up a copy of her groundbreaking research, *Positivity!*

Resilient people have the ability to shift gears and let go. The reason some people don't possess brilliant resilience is they hold on to things long after others have moved on.

The following tool will help you reflect on the milestones in your journey so far that have brought you to your current state of believing and being. Take a glimpse in your rearview mirror and spend a few minutes working through these eight questions.

The Rearview Mirror

1. What aspects of your life have been most rewarding to you thus far? What has brought you joy?

_____

_____

_____

2. What times in your life did you find the most challenging? What has brought you sorrow?

_____

_____

_____

3. How did these best and worst of times shape your values and choices?

_____

_____

_____

4. Which people have been most significant in your journey thus far and how so?

_____

_____

_____

5. How did these people influence your choices? Your feeling of self-worth?

_____

_____

_____

6. What have been some major turning points in your life, ex-
    pected or unexpected?

_____

_____

_____

7. What significant contributions do you feel you have made
    to date?

_____

_____

_____

8. What have been your major lessons?

_____

_____

_____

Look Sideways

Whether you are looking to shift personally or professionally,
the bottom line is this: regardless of your situation, you *can* change
the way you look at things. You can shift out of neutral—out of
the ordinary and into the extraordinary. And when you shift into
your brilliance, it allows those on either side of you to release their
own brilliance. Then they, too, will begin to see things with a fresh
mind. If you aren't where you want to be or find yourself stalled, it
may be time to look at things in a sideways or cockeyed way.

Here's an example. Did you know that NASA designed a
fascinating experiment to test the physiological impact of spatial
disorientation, the kind astronauts experience when they have spent
an extended period of time in a weightless environment? A group
of astronaut candidates was outfitted with convex goggles that

flipped everything in their field of vision 180 degrees, so that the world they saw was completely upside down. The subjects wore the glasses 24 hours a day, even when they slept.

At first, the astronaut candidates experienced great stress and anxiety, which lingered for many days. But 26 days after the experiment began, an amazing thing happened to one of the subjects. His world turned right-side up again! His goggles were the same as the others', and he was wearing them all the time just as they were. But what had happened was that his brain, with all of this new input, had "rewired" itself and made new neural connections that enabled him to "right what had been wrong." Within a few days, *all* the other astronauts experienced the same phenomenon!

This experiment of seeing something differently led to break-through discoveries and lucid vision. What had been distressing and disorienting became clear and comfortable. I'm not suggesting that you need to hop on the next shuttle to the moon in order to change your perspective. But you can rewire your thoughts to see options, and trust nature to adjust along with you. Now, that's Vujá dé!

Look Forward

Naturally, a car windshield is much larger than either the side mirrors or the rearview mirror. We're meant to focus more on what's in front of us than what is behind us. We're meant to look ahead, to see what's coming, what's around the corner.

As important as it is to reflect on how your past experiences have shaped your present and challenge your view every now and then, you must also look beyond today and envision the possibilities.

People generally know so much about what they know that they are the last to see the future differently. —Edie Weiner

Here are two important strategies for envisioning your future:

- Clear Your Vision
- Sharpen Your Focus

Clear Your Vision

Have you ever jumped in your car, started down the road, and discovered your windshield was dirty? Maybe it was smudged with tree sap, bird droppings, or worse—the equivalent of Florida love bugs? Washing fluid and wiper blades in motion just don't cut it. You have to stop, get out of the car, and scrape off those pesky smears that blur your vision.

The same goes for some of the "mess" that gets on your personal window of life—the naysayers, the sticky situations, and other barriers that require an extra effort to clear away so you can see where you are headed.

Your vision represents your expectations for the future. Seeing differently requires opening your eyes *and* your mind to the possibilities that lie before you. You must use your imagination to envision the future YOU.

Our imagination is the most powerful video production facility in the world. In fact, everything that exists on the face of the earth was first a picture in the mind of the creator.

Let's test this. What are you daydreaming about right now? Do you expect joy, abundance, and prosperity? Or disappointment, emptiness, and failure?

Every hope, wish, desire, and dream is birthed in the imagination. When your mother carried you in her womb, she began to imagine what you would look like. When you start planning your vacation—which some of you desperately need—perhaps you imagine yourself hiking through a cool forest, shushing down pristine slopes, or lying on the beach soaking up the sun's rays.

You are the sum total of every image that has been displayed on the movie screen of your mind. You will never rise above the image you have of yourself in your mind. If you want to change where you're going in life, then you have to change what you're seeing in your imagination.

The universe is waiting for you to imagine a life that is so big the hair on the back of your neck will stand up. The trick with personal visions, however, is that they must be both ambitious and realistic. Here are a few simple steps to help you clear your vision and keep it that way:

Five Steps to Clear Your Vision	
See it!	Visualize who you want to be and what you want your life to be like. The picture that resides in your imagination will happen before you know it.
Write it!	Take the picture that's in your mind and put words, expressions, and feelings to it. Then put it down on paper!
Read it!	When you wake up each morning, read your vision aloud and meditate on it. Before your head hits the pillow at night, read it and meditate on it again.
Say it!	When you speak your vision, say it with power, emotion, and conviction.
Act it!	Start believing, behaving, and acting as if your vision has already come true…and begin doing it today. Don't wait for tomorrow or sometime in the future. When you arrive in the future, you will reap everything that you've sown in the past.

Write it: The Three C's of a Clear Vision Statement

I emphasize the need to write down your vision so it can become more than an abstract idea—so it can have life and become an action. And writing it is also a good way to share it with others, which, in turn, will allow them to hold you accountable for fulfilling that vision. When you decide to write your vision statement, follow these steps as a reminder of what is possible in your life.

CLEAR

What do I want?

_____

_____

_____

Where am I going with this goal/dream?

_____

_____

_____

CANDID

Why am I doing this?

_____

_____

_____

What should I expect to change?

_____

_____

_____

What can I handle on my own, and what help do I need from others?

_____

_____

_____

COMPELLING

What are the possibilities?

_____

_____

_____

What is the personal payoff?

_____

_____

_____

What are the benefits to others?

_____

_____

_____

My Personal Vision Statement

_____

_____

_____

_____

_____

_____

_____

Simon T. Says... Relax and take a deep
breath. Create a clear and compelling vision
that answers the following questions:

- What is the most important thing you must do daily/weekly to stay intellectually stimulated?

- What outlet do you immerse yourself in to stay connected to the issues of the day?

- Who is challenging you to become the best you can be?

- What is one thing that you would like to accomplish in your business within the next 30 days?

Sharpen Your Focus

- Shifting your brilliance and seeing differently require a sharp sense of focus. Focus is the ability to identify an important goal or vision and to channel your efforts toward specific actions that support achieving that goal or vision. It's like turning on the high beams when driving in the dark or turning on a spotlight to focus on what really drives performance. David Evans, author of *Dare to Be a Man,* says, "Your goals choose your actions, decisions, relationships, leaders, teachers, and mentors." Without focused thought and energy put toward a well-defined vision, you have little chance of seeing anything of value come to fruition.

- When you set new goals or create a new vision for your life, your focus is typically clear at the onset. But over time, that focus and your energy can become scattered. No matter what role you play, whether in your personal or professional setting, all day you are bombarded with multiple messages, competing priorities, and pressing issues that need your undivided attention. Life has gotten complex, and it takes a clear line of sight to stay on course.

- It may be time to turn up your high beams to increase your capacity to focus. It's easy to lose sight or become distracted thinking about all the things you could or should be doing. Learning to focus on the important items will move you toward your vision.

- Shifting *effectively* requires focusing on the right things at the right time. All too often, we allow people, circumstances, and events to distort our perspective and our vision. What actions do you need to take to get back on track to where you want to go, who you want to become, and what you want to do? Try the following strategies to sharpen your focus.

I don't skate to where the puck is; I skate to where the puck is going to be. —Wayne Gretsky

---

Strategies for Sharpening Your Focus

- Work to reduce or eliminate disruptions.
- Use good personal organization and time management skills.
- Commit to directing your energy at key targets.
- Ensure all activities are aligned with desired results.
- Devote the majority of time to the top 20% of the priority list.

- Stay fully alert.

- Eliminate waste.

- Show the power of resistance: learn to say no.

- Anticipate surprises.

- Beware of the dangers of multitasking.

- Hone your discerning skills.

- Improve your self-discipline.

- Become familiar with your personal concentration threshold.

- Know your own derailers.

HARNESS THE POWER OF YOU, INC.

When Wall Street lists a stock on the New York Stock Exchange or the NASDAQ, it must meet a minimum of standards. Analysts issue a buy, hold, or sell on a stock based on the projection of future value growth by industry, market, and numerous other factors. In order for a stock to maintain a "buy" status and prevent it being delisted, it must continue to meet the standards to ensure investors that it is a credible investment. It makes no difference the length of time it has been listed or the numerous fluctuations in the market.

Now, when you joined your company, they invested in a stock called You, Inc. They invested in your talent, education, experience, and potential for future growth. In other words, they made a BET (Brilliance, Energy, and Time) on you. What will you do to make sure they receive a handsome payoff?

The bottom line is that your organization wants high performance from you. It wants an employee who is an asset (something of value) rather than a liability (something that is a disadvantage or a drawback).

Your CEO must continually create value for and answer to the stockholders, shareholders, and stakeholders who have a vested interest in your organization. And there's a good chance that outside consultants are whispering in your CEO's ear, suggesting that profits per employee be increased. Of course, one way to improve profit per employee is to simply get rid of low-profit employees. Another way is to increase the number of high-profit employees.

In the book *Mobilizing Minds* by McKinsey & Company, consultants Lowell Bryan and Claudia Joyce's, research shows that in 1984, General Electric employed 330,000 people, and about 20% of those were either managers or professionals. By 2004, GE had reduced its workforce to 307,000, but the percentage of professionals and leaders had increased to 55%—an increase of approximately *100,000* professionals and managerial types! As a result, GE's profit per employee per year more than quadrupled, from $12,500 in 1984 to $54,000 in 2004. In addition, its market capitalization increased from $47 billion to $386 billion (that's 825%!), while its book equity increased 482%.

In an interview, Jack Welch, former Chairman and CEO of GE, told about a private equity firm that acquired a business doing $12 billion annually with 26,000 employees. He said that in a few short years it would generate the same revenue with only 14,000 employees. Please read the tea leaves, my friend. If you don't compound your stock portfolio of ideas, value, and potential growth, you will be delisted and downgraded.

The reason you face so much scrutiny in your job is that Big Brother needs to know whether you are making them money or costing them. That's why I strongly advise you to see yourself as a self-employed employee who is responsible for bringing value and productivity to the marketplace. Take control of your future by deploying your best thinking in growing yourself every day.

As I explored in *Release Your Brilliance*, each of us is born brilliant—with special talents and genius in a deep vault within. And when we release our brilliance, we shift from waiting for the future to arrive to creating it every day by our actions. The potential to be CEO of You, Inc. already exists within each of us. So how do you harness this internal power? And how do you let it out?

Draw confidence from your personal gifts and talents by doing a quarterly assessment of your career/business portfolio. Examine your personal productivity, relationship currency, and skills inventory.

Here are three strategies to harness your power:

- Believe in Your Worth
- Think *Inside* the Box
- Distinguish Thyself

Believe in Your Worth

I once heard a story about the famous painter Pablo Picasso. He was dining at a five-star restaurant in a metropolitan city when a female admirer walked over to his table to tell him how much she loved his work. Sensing that he was receptive to her accolades, she asked if he would do a sketch for her. Picasso grabbed some paper and, with pen and pencil, promptly depicted the waiters carrying luscious ice cream parfaits. As the woman reached for the sketch, Picasso said, "Madame, that will be $10,000." Shocked, the woman replied, "But that only took you five minutes." "No, Madame," replied Picasso, "it took me 50 years."

Simon T. Says... Dare to shift gears and see things differently when others are stalled.

To shift your brilliance, whether in your personal or professional life, you need to live life with bold confidence so you don't diminish your value. You need to believe in your own merit, regardless of what flaws you may have or what challenges you face. When you believe in your innate brilliance, you will find the confidence to take action.

Confidence comes from believing in your own self-worth. It's living out loud. It is the voice within that says, "I can, I shall, I will!" Confidence is the ability to go in your own direction instead of following the crowd. Confidence is your own quiet power. Without confidence, there is no ignition; there is no dream come true; there is no better tomorrow.

Confidence comes from hours and days and weeks
and years of constant work and dedication.
—Roger Staubach, Hall of Fame Quarterback Dallas Cowboys

Why would Microsoft make a bid to buy Yahoo? Confidence. Why would Richard Branson launch an airline called Virgin America? Confidence. Why would Sheila Robinson start Diversity Woman, a leadership empowerment online magazine for women who mean business? Confidence, my friend.

The problem for most of us is that confidence, the very thing we need the most these days, is in short supply. Our self-assurance has come under severe attack as a result of the reeling economy, layoffs, hiring freezes, cancelled contracts, reduction of benefits—the list goes on.

I was in Washington, DC, recently, enjoying a chai latte at one of the world's favorite coffee spots (Starbucks, of course) and having a fascinating conversation with a friend, Lana Kim, who is a political refugee from Russia. She was telling me about her latest endeavor—writing a book. When I asked her why she hadn't done it sooner, she replied, "Simon, I lacked the confidence; I didn't believe I really could do it."

Let me tell you about Lana Kim. She came to America alone, with just a dollar in her pocket and no knowledge of the English language. Despite unbelievable difficulties, through years of hard work and self-education, she became a stockbroker and was actually inducted into the hall of fame in that role at PaineWebber. Today, she is also a Certified Financial Planner (CFP), a Registered Financial Consultant (RFC), and is completing her Master of Science degree in financial services. And this brilliant woman, who has achieved so much against all odds, was sitting there telling me she lacked confidence.

In her own words:

> I had struggled nearly 35 years to have confidence, a gleam of hope, a belief that I could be somebody and make my life count for something. What I've learned is that confidence grows with you one day at a time, one encounter at a time.

Lana worked every day to boost her confidence by reading motivational books, listening to tapes, making new friends, and volunteering. But most importantly, she began to believe in her own worth. What about you?

Think *Inside* the Box

Power resides inside the box. Where in our cars do we keep our most valuable goods such as our registration, owner's manual, maybe even our money or keys? Inside the glove box.

To make any kind of change in your life, you must be able to draw strength and affirmation from inside your own box. Too many people are dependent on external recognition. Do you ever wonder if major athletes play to win or play to please the crowd or someone in particular in the crowd? Think about performers in general. What happens to their egos when they don't receive a standing ovation, or make the blockbuster film, or sell out the seats in the arena?

Simon T. Says: Power resides inside the box.

With a little clicking on Google, I uncovered the studies by Professor Andrew Hargadon at the Graduate School of Management at the University of California, Davis. According to Hargadon:

> The term "out-of-the-box thinking" came from solutions to the so-called "nine dot problem"—where there are three rows of three dots and the problem is to connect all the dots with just four lines—without lifting the pen. The solution lies in drawing a line that goes outside the imaginary "box" formed by those nine dots. "Thinking out of the box" has come to mean thinking of a solution that is somehow outside of what you already know and do, coming up with something wholly new.

Okay, I know what you're doing right now…you just took out a pen and some paper to try this exercise.

That's what I did when I first read Hargadon's summation. But the point is we've taken this idea of thinking outside the box to the extreme.

The notion that we have to look outside of ourselves to find something fresh, creative, or remarkable is quite simply not true! It minimizes our inherent genius and discounts all the learning, wisdom, and experience we've gained through hard work, trial and error, and past experiences. I say all the time, "Most of what you need to succeed is already inside of you." Of course we occasionally need to look for solutions outside the realm of our current knowledge, but to disregard and ignore our known internal brilliance is like turning our backs on acres of diamonds buried in our own backyards. (If you're not familiar with that phrase, I encourage you to read R.H. Conwell's magical little book, *Acres of Diamonds*.)

As a business thought leader who helps organizations and individuals remove hidden barriers to increased productivity, I used to feel the need to connect with people to feel praiseworthy. I needed to be needed. If no one reached out to me, I'd begin to wonder if something was wrong. Fortunately, I came to a place where I can now look within for my recognition. I realize that I don't have to talk to someone every day (or hear myself talk, for that matter) to feel I add value.

Simon T. Says... Most of what you need
to succeed is already inside of you.

Distinguish Thyself

A dear friend of mine, Sylvia Weinstock, known as the Leonardo da Vinci of cakes, said: "I am an artist who is commissioned to create a work of art. Everything that I do is original and unrepeatable. Flour, sugar, and water are only limited by one's imagination."

Why do I mention Sylvia? Because she has distinguished herself. According to Dictionary.com, the word "distinct" is described as unquestionably exceptional or notable. Are those words used to describe you, O Brilliant One?

This is the time for you to professionally distinguish your work, product, service, and brand! If you work for someone else, then you are a brand inside a brand. If you own your own business, then you are a brand.

David McNally and Karl Speak, authors of *Be Your Own Brand*, say, "A brand is not a product or service. It's an emotion, a perception, a memory, an experience. You mean something to everyone in your life, and that meaning is your brand." Seth Godin, author and thought leader, says, "A brand is a way of identifying and communicating what makes you a star, and using those qualities to separate yourself from the herd will increase your success."

Think about it this way. Do you know people with average looks, average skills, and average backgrounds who possess the "It Factor"? They walk into a room and instantly light it up. They make releasing their brilliance look easy. Good things constantly happen to them, and they seem to always land on their feet. Why are they special? What makes them different?

These people have an aura that supersedes what you see on the outside. The word "aura," which is of Latin origin and first appeared in the 14th century, means *gentle breeze* or *breath of air*. In the 19th century, the definition expanded to mean *emanation or atmosphere*.

Your brand aura is your signature presence. It's what distinguishes you from everyone else. When you tap into and release your authentic self, you become a breath of fresh air. You breathe vibrant life and energy into everyone you meet and everything you put your hands to. You have the power to literally change the atmosphere around you.

Here are a few examples:

- I mentioned the television drama *Scandal* earlier. Well, it's impossible to ignore the rags to riches story of the creator of *Scandal* and *Grey's Anatomy*, writer Shonda Rhimes. Recently voted one of Forbes 50 most powerful women, she went from an unknown starving artist writing in her pajamas at home just a few years ago to arguably television's most well-known success story. Although she's rarely in the forefront by choice, Shonda is a perfect example of how excellence in your unique gift or talent can alone define your brand aura and be the conduit through which you shift your brilliance.

- Celine Dion was quoted as saying, "If God could sing, He would sound a lot like Andrea Bocelli." When we talk about harnessing your inner power—living in the power of your own aura—there are few who exemplify this as well as this legendary Italian tenor. Bocelli lost his eyesight as an adolescent, and in turn, discovered new, brilliant sensibilities that transcended his physical limitation. He was able to "see differently" the interpretation of lyrics and his perception of musical expression, and it's apparent in the unique sound that's become his signature. Since his humble start being discovered at a singing competition just shy of two decades ago to his status today as the biggest-selling artist in the history of classical music, he has sold more than 80 million records worldwide. Marketing and Public Relations efforts could not have contrived the degree of connection Bocelli has with his audience and the level of exponential success he's achieved. The pure, unadulterated, and extraordinary gift of his romantic tenor voice has created a signature presence like this world has never seen.

What Bocelli and Rhimes have in common is that they once were considered average or even disadvantaged in some way, but they took ordinary opportunities, breathed life into them, and then created something extraordinary. That's why everyone talks about them. This is what your place of business wants you to do, to be extraordinary so everyone sees your brilliance.

Having a brilliant aura is not a privilege reserved for the famous. All around you are people who glow, who exhibit a signature presence. Think about it: weren't there kids in your high school or college who always stood out, who had that special something? And aren't these the same individuals everyone asks about at reunions? Even then, these people had an essence that caused others to want to be around them. Those who possess the "It Factor" are not merely lucky. They confidently and purposefully use their signature presence to shift! They allow their brilliance and their spirit to be the power that transports them into the future they desire. They let their Vujá dé guide them onward.

Here are some ways to distinguish yourself:

- Increase your business acumen. Understand the industry of your company, its competitors, and its brand position in the marketplace, products, and services.

- Share with your customers what you will do to earn or keep their business! They don't really care about what you can't do or all the hoops you have to jump through to make something happen. Be straight up and stop playing the head games. In the words of Verizon, *"Be the Reason"* they stay with your organization.

- Establish a personal Board of Directors made up of men and women who "get you" and will challenge you in the eight core areas of your life—spiritual, family, career, financial, emotional, mental, social, and wellness. Plan to meet with them every 90 days to discuss what you have done to grow your brand and distinguish yourself from the rest of the pack.

- Diversify your circles of influence. If everyone in your circle looks like you, talks like you, and thinks like you, then your circle is too small.

Hungry for even more ways to shift your brilliance? Visit www.shiftyourbrilliance.com to connect, share, and learn how to sustain your brilliance.

In order to distinguish yourself, you need to know and develop your own inner power. Answer the following questions to examine that power.

Inner Power Reflection

1. What gives me confidence?

_____

_____

_____

2. What are three of my unique talents?

_____

_____

_____

3. How do I get affirmation of my worth?

_____

_____

_____

4. I believe I add value because…

_____

_____

_____

5. Three words that describe my personal signature are:

_____

_____

_____

Tips for Boosting Your Aura

Increase your self-talk. Every morning as you prepare for your day, say aloud seven times, "I am brilliant, happy, healthy, and whole in my soul." Watch what happens inside you and around you.

Explore ways to change the atmosphere around you. Start with some simple steps: Be positive and self-confident, smile, state your name, or give a compliment. When you walk into a room, "own" it. Enliven every place you go with a warm hello, a sincere thank you in the form of a handwritten note or thoughtful e-card, and a memorable goodbye.

Examine your partnering skills and look for ways to collaborate. If someone asks you for help, give of yourself with joy and an engaging spirit. Consider how you want others to respond when you ask for assistance. The law of reciprocity is powerful. Use it.

Check your voicemail greeting. Is it boring? Change it—it's your brand speaking loud and clear. Your ringtone is a clear indication of how you want people to think about you, but be sure it represents you as a professional.

Keep your personal life personal. No one really cares that you got drunk over the weekend or did whatever. It will sometimes cause people to wonder if you are mentally and physically fit as a corporate athlete. Beware of TMI (Too Much Information).

Reinvent yourself. While what's inside matters most, a good polish never hurts. Perhaps it's time for an extreme professional makeover. Start with the one big thing you could do that would make you more marketable, and go from there.

Try these little ideas as well:

- Dress for the job you intend to occupy one day.

- Make people laugh.

- Have an opinion about everything (but keep an open mind).

- Hand out an unusual business card.

- Recast your resume to stand out.

- Take up an unusual hobby.

- Build visibility by raising your profile.

- Keep your vibe alive!

IGNITE A FRESH VISION

Stale…stuck…spiritless. That is what an organization becomes when it loses its mojo.

Simply launching a new product in this hypersensitive, over-communicative society isn't enough anymore. Opening a new building and hanging a sign out front is old and tired. Marketing to people through the "three screens"—television, computer, mobile phone—has lost its impact because people now have the power to immediately TiVo or delete you out of their space.

According to Kevin Roberts, CEO Worldwide, of Saatchi & Saatchi, "You've got three seconds to impress me (the customer), three seconds to connect with me, to make me fall in love with your product." That's all you have, O Brilliant One—three seconds.

The moment customers interact with your organization, they will instantly judge if it is an authentic experience or the same old dry, dull, disjointed encounter. In their minds, it's been there, done that.

Don't look for extraordinary people; build a place where
ordinary people can do extraordinary things. —Keith
McFarland, author of *The Breakthrough Company*

In my travels, I observe organizations that spend untold hundreds of millions of dollars reinvigorating themselves. Often, after launching the new television/Internet commercial, shifting their collateral material from paper to online, and announcing to the world that they are "new and improved," customers experience and know the truth: it's old wine in new skin.

Meanwhile, everyone inside the organization is waiting for sparks to fly and be launched into the stratosphere. Yet in a few months' time, reality sets in and the brand "star" comes crashing back to earth. Why does this happen? Because too many organizations and leaders believe that reinvigorating with a new vision is a top-down rather than a bottom-up proposition. There is very little room, if any, for shifts in brilliance. I know that those who work in the executive suites are supposed to have all of the answers because they're paid the big bucks, right?

Well, truth be told, the employees who are closest to the customers have some of the answers. However, if you never talk to them—never solicit their input—and only tell them what to do, they will disown your vision because they won't feel the vision promise in their gut. Instead of being passionate champions, they operate under the belief, "I'll just do my job and be gone, because leadership doesn't care about me, nor do they truly believe in giving us an ownership stake."

To ignite a fresh vision that enables customers to achieve their goals, your brand vision must live in the hearts and minds of every team member, from the front line to the executive suite. If your vision thrives and stands the test of time, it will do so because each individual feels a significant sense of ownership.

Shifting yourself and creating the future is a marathon, not a sprint. According to Rosabeth Moss-Kanter, former editor of the *Harvard Business Review*, "Lasting change is not supported by quick, bold strokes, but rather by focused, sustained marches." Change must take place at every level of the organization in the form of a personal commitment by every team member. This enables a vision to have stickiness and to be lived from the inside out.

Charles Schwab was one of the first managers to win a salary of $1,000,000 annually in the 1920s. He ran Andrew Carnegie's United States Steel Company. Under Schwab's direction, U.S. Steel was absolute tops in the industry for its day. What was Schwab's secret? He said, "I consider my ability to arouse enthusiasm among my people the greatest asset I possess." The way to develop the best in a person is by understanding their vision and motivation for success. Now, that's a shift of brilliance.

Try these methods to ignite your passion:

- Mine Your Motivator
- Commit Emotionally
- Be a Chief Breakthrough Officer

There are lots of tips, tools, and techniques in our blog to keep your passion ignited. Go to www.simontbailey.com.

Mine Your Motivator

To ignite a vision, you must do the inner work to discover what motivates you—the source of your energy. Some of you may be aware of a term "gumption trap," which Robert Pirsig coined in his famous 1974 best seller, *Zen and the Art of Motorcycle Maintenance.*

This term refers to a mindset that causes a person to lose enthusiasm and discourages him/her from starting or finishing a project. The book describes a 17-day motorcycle journey across the United States by the author, his son, and two close friends. It contrasts personality types, those interested mostly in romantic notions and those who are rationally analytic and need to know the details. This contrast comes to light in the divergent ways the characters go about repairing (or not) their motorcycles. It eventually becomes apparent that motorcycle maintenance may be tedious or pleasurable, depending on one's attitude.

What motivates you today gives you the currency to
purchase what you will be tomorrow. Today's advantages
must be used to buy tomorrow's opportunities.
—Mensa Otabil, author of *Buy the Future*

This metaphor of having gumption has become a popular method of illustrating the importance and the effect of having a genuine passion for something.

Every person is motivated by something in particular...maybe not motorcycle maintenance, but who knows? When you know what motivates you, life becomes an exciting adventure. You are driven by your passion, and you have a reason for getting out of bed in the morning. This kind of energy is natural and essential for personal success.

My primary motivator happens to be "the difference that makes the difference." I realized a long time ago that I am here on Earth to serve and advise people. Serving and advising aren't always about telling people what to do; more often than not, they involve asking people what they are thinking and listening to their responses. To me, that is being a difference maker. I consider it my universal assignment to inspire, impact, infuse, enlighten, and encourage one individual, one business, or one company at a time. I am fortunate enough to get confirmation from clients, associates, and others that my "work is working." I know what my gumption is.

Mine Your Motivator Tool

This tool will help you drill down to unearth your primary motivator. It will help you find out what really sets you on fire, what makes your hair blow back, and the nape of your neck tingle.

Part One

1. Ask yourself what kinds of motivators, or payoffs, you seek in anything you do. For example, you may get a sense of satisfaction by making a difference, by helping people, or by overcoming barriers to meet a goal.

_____

_____

_____

2. To get you thinking, review the list of drivers, or motivators, shown following Part Three, and circle *seven* that speak to you as the ones that impact you most.

Part Two

3. Review the seven choices you circled and select the *top three* that most motivate you, and record them in the space below.

_____

_____

_____

4. Examine your top three motivators and select *the one* that you consider your core motivator. Record it in the triangle below.

Part Three

5. How does knowing your core motivator help you commit to your personal best?

_____

_____

_____

6. What can you do more of?

_____

_____

_____

7. How will knowing your core motivator help you begin to shift toward your goals?

_____

_____

8. What can you do more of?

_____

_____

_____

KEY MOTIVATORS

Communicate	Organize	Solve	Collaborate	Achieve
Inspire	Fulfill	Confidence	Connect	Cause
Big picture	Assemble	Be aware	Bond	Empower
Attract	Accomplish	Be present	Coach	Increase
Engage	Build	Unified	Comfort	Direct
Emphasize	Opportunity	Courage	Fun	Excellence
Reflect	Ignite	Impact	Humor	Distinguish
Listen	Develop	Elegance	Congruent	Encourage
Entertain	Prioritize	Mutual	Energy	Execute
Enlighten	Detail-oriented	Create awareness	Exhilaration	Experiment
Accurate	Finish	Honesty	Unleash	Risk
Empathize	Dedicate	Improve	Honor	Ethical
Foster	Invent	Understand	In touch	Influence
Complete	Master	Recognize	Integrate	Imagine
Truthful	Integrity	Earn the right	Learn	Add value
Administer	Relevant	Discover	Mentor	Purpose
Explain	Create	Make better	Assist	Accept challenge
Tell a story	Lead	Adjust	Experience	Transform
Visionary	Quest	Win-win	Contribute	Best practice
Leave a legacy	Produce	Forward momentum	Appreciate	Make a difference

Commit Emotionally

Another very important aspect of igniting your passion is making an emotional commitment...on top of a rational one. What is the difference? Rational commitment is the "what" you agree to give an organization when you're hired—your time and energy in exchange for financial compensation, professional development, and a chance to fulfill your career ambitions. Emotional commitment is the "why"—the passion and the purpose behind the work. It's what keeps you in the relationship with the organization. When you are emotionally committed, your confidence increases and your heart flutters with complete satisfaction as you enjoy your professional utopia.

According to a study by the Corporate Leadership Council, emotional commitment drives discretionary effort. The authors surveyed 50,000 employees from 59 different organizations in 27 countries, representing ten industry groups. They revealed that discretionary effort means being willing to take on more work, offering to assist others when they are overloaded, or going the extra mile without anyone asking.

I vividly remember the day I decided to step up to the plate and committed emotionally to something very important to me. I had just received an unsolicited kiss from my four-year-old daughter, Madison. Man, I lit up like a Christmas tree. That sweet, innocent kiss touched my very soul. At that moment, I ached with love for my beautiful daughter, but realized sadly that I really didn't know how to raise her. I didn't have all the answers and was pretty sure I was never going to have them. Suddenly I felt stunned and totally humbled that she had been entrusted to my care until she became an independent adult. I understood for the first time the powerful truth that I was the person, along with her mother, who would teach her the meaning of being a good woman, a decent person, whether intentionally or not. I was the model, the imprint she would carry around in her heart and mind for the rest of her life.

At that moment I became not just a father, but an *intentional* father. I decided to accept the awesome responsibility of being Madison's parent wholeheartedly, no matter what it brought. I would do my utmost to provide for her. I vowed to spend time with her no matter how busy my schedule. I promised to talk to her, to model the qualities that I felt a noble, moral man (and parent) should have. That's what being committed emotionally has meant for me. And it has made all of the difference.

Emotional Commitment Pulse Check

Respond to the following questions to assess your own emotional commitments.

	Low				High
1. What is your current level of emotional commitment to your friendships?	1	2	3	4	5
2. What is your current level of emotional commitment to your community?	1	2	3	4	5
3. What is your current level of emotional commitment to your hobbies and special interests?	1	2	3	4	5
4. What is your current level of emotional commitment to your immediate family?	1	2	3	4	5
5. What is your current level of emotional commitment to becoming a shifter?	1	2	3	4	5

What can you do personally to increase your emotional commitment?

_____

_____

_____

> Rationally committed people do what they **have** to do.
> Emotionally committed people do what they **love** to do.

Tips for Emotional Commitment

- Raise your hand and volunteer to help instead of waiting.

- Know what matters most to you and those closest to you.

- Put your heart and soul into everything you do.

- Be proactive; go the extra mile.

Be a Chief Breakthrough Officer (CBO)

After every break-up, there is a breakdown. And after the breakdown, there is a breakthrough. When you tap into your passion, you will inevitably find yourself in a creative place, enjoying your work, and embracing your life. All this positive energy will inevitably lead to new discoveries, new ideas, and new solutions to old problems.

I was recently in the Delta Sky Club in Atlanta and happened to pick up a magazine. Inside was an advertisement to be a CBO (Chief Breakthrough Officer) by attending an executive course offered at the Stanford Graduate School of Business.

We live in a knowledge economy. Organizations realize that their competitive edge lies in what their people have between their ears. Innovation is found within the minds of human beings.

Indra Nooyi, Chairman and CEO of PepsiCo, the largest food and beverage company in the U.S., has also officially earned the title of CBO. After years of plummeting shares and profits, the company saw record highs under her leadership after a breakthrough of reinvention. Did Indra and the PepsiCo leadership team revive the business by resting upon the old success of the flat domestic soda business on which the company was built? Absolutely not. The innovative thinking of the company's leaders and other collective intelligence led to a shift toward fast-growing but unfamiliar product territories like yogurt and hummus. Today, PepsiCo has employed Vujá dé thinking to the tune of 22 different billion-dollar brands.

What power can you conjure up, what passion can you tap into to get the job done?

A friend of mine approached a leader of the company she works for about shifting her role to one with greater responsibility. She wanted to focus on being a sales and technology trainer. Why? As a result of her tenure at the company, most people were coming to her on a regular basis to ask questions about contracts and how to best leverage the software to drive more revenue. She also noticed that there were many new sales people who didn't know how to dress, didn't understand e-mail etiquette, didn't know how to make a customer sales call, etc. She soon recognized that the greatest value she could bring would be to create a standardized training program for the sales team.

She also knew that companies that spend $900 per employee on learning and development experience 57% higher net sales per employee, 37% higher gross profits per employee, and a 20% higher ratio in market-to-book values, according to the American

Society of Training and Development. She was willing to see this through the lens of Vujá dé—a vision for the future—and she was emotionally committed to making it work.

Another example of a Chief Breakthrough Officer is Facebook's COO Sheryl Sandberg, author of best-selling book *Lean In: Women, Work, and the Will to Lead,* which has sparked a movement for the creation of a gender equitable society and made her a global celebrity. The lean in movement aims to help women achieve their personal and professional goals. Under her leadership, Facebook is now in the mobile computing game, earning the company $2 of every $5 in revenue from mobile versus $0 earned the year before the launch.

> Reasonable people adapt themselves to the world.
> Unreasonable people attempt to adapt the world
> to themselves. All progress, therefore, depends on
> unreasonable people. —George Bernard Shaw

Many organizations such as those referenced are in need of employees who have cross-functional skills. They are looking for people who display myriad-minded abilities in areas such as leadership, strategy planning, financial literacy, marketing and sales, strategic relationships, negotiation, technology, and operational management. In fact, in a recent IBM study of 1,500 corporate heads and public sector leaders across 60 nations and 33 industries on what drives them in managing their companies in today's world, it was revealed that the number one leadership quality they are looking for is creativity.

As Ronald Baker, founder of the VeraSage Institute, pointed out in *Talent* magazine:

Characteristics such as passion, desire, obsession, motivation, innovation, creativity, and knowledge may not show up anywhere on financial statements, but they are the traits that will ultimately determine the fate of the company. This attitude does not fit well with more common command-and-control hierarchies, but it will become an essential mind-shift in the 21st century if organizations are to reap the wealth-creating possibilities of knowledge workers.

You, too, can be a CBO of your life or your organization. What challenges are you or your business facing? Remember, after every breakdown, there is a breakthrough. Become the breakthrough your company has been waiting for. How can you be a CBO at home? What can you systematize to make things run more smoothly for the family? Or for yourself, when it comes to errands, meals, and home repair?

> Uncommon people do uncommon things during uncommon times. It doesn't make sense to hire smart people and then tell them what to do; we hire smart people so they can tell us what to do. —Steve Jobs, Founder, *Apple*

Challenge yourself to try new ways of doing routine things. Maybe a breakthrough is what you need to shift in your daily living. Try some of the following tips.

How to Be a CBO

- Don't settle for business as usual. Ask bigger questions.
- Stay current with what affects your business or surrounding community. What isn't working anymore?

- Obtain a copy of your company's annual report and discover what drives the organization. Learn the language that is used to describe how different lines of business are doing.

- If your company is privately held, ask your manager to set up a mentoring visit for you and another leader. Be prepared to ask insightful questions to get a better view about how you can make a difference.

- Be curious about everything. Find out more: What's the story behind the story? The need behind the need?

- Volunteer on a project team that is tackling an issue that impacts your department, division, or organization as a whole.

- Invest in yourself by subscribing to GetAbstract.com, which is the iTunes of business books. It has over 5,000 business book summaries on topics such as branding, creativity, innovation, and customer loyalty. If you like what you read, invest in the entire book.

- Create a list of best practices, shortcuts, insights, and workarounds that have saved time and money in your current position. Ask others for their lists, too.

- Take risks and welcome new challenges: accept out-of-state/overseas positions or assignments in areas that are unfamiliar to you.

Shift Your Brilliance Moment: Go to www.simontbailey.com and look for tips, tools, and techniques in our blog.

FUEL YOUR MIND

Once you have harnessed your courage and ignited a fresh vision, it's time to fuel your mind. If you are truly committed to experiencing a shift in your brilliance, then you must take responsibility for your own growth and development and for the unleashing of your potential.

According to recent research, about 90% of life is lived in the subconscious realm, while only 10% is lived in the conscious dimension. What this means is that many powerful beliefs have been driven into our minds, and we don't even know they are there. We have no idea how profoundly they influence our words, our thinking, our actions, and our behaviors.

While maybe it's not as much of a problem these days, many of us have had the experience of driving down the road and hearing that metallic sound and hollow knocking. Remember that? "Bad gas" it was called. These pinging noises were caused by improper octane levels, an overly lean air-to-fuel mixture, or a lack of proper exhaust gas recirculation.

In the same way, people sometimes fuel their minds with "poor mixtures." We fill up with others' dire opinions—what one may call "head trash"—adopting prejudices or limited views of certain issues. This kind of thinking can cripple your future. To shift in the right direction, you want to fill your mind with positive, productive thoughts, not useless, negative gossip or speculation.

Follow these simple strategies to fuel your mind:

- See Your Tank as Half Full (Not Half Empty!)
- Choose Only High-Grade Relationships
- Beware the Backseat Drivers
- Expand Your Network
- Find a Mentor
- Be a Lifelong Learner

See Your Tank as Half Full (Not Half Empty!)

Even though my job demands that I stay positive, there have been moments in the past year when I felt discouraged and disappointed. A few times I questioned everything and found myself being quietly negative. If people tell you they are always positive and never experience bad days, they are lying.

Optimism, as defined by Dictionary.com, is the tendency to expect the best possible outcome or dwell on the most hopeful aspects of a situation. We're all familiar with the old adage of seeing the glass half full. To fuel your mind with the right kind of thinking, you need to adopt a half full (not half empty) mentality.

Have you ever thought about where your beliefs come from? Many of them are formulated during childhood when we unquestioningly accepted the opinions—both helpful and harmful, both true and false—of the influential people in our lives. Feelings are created when we hear, see, or experience something that leaves an imprint on our brains, and a corresponding belief is downloaded into our subconscious minds.

Unfortunately, most of us pick up more on the negative imprints of our pasts, causing us to lack confidence in our abilities. We tend to doubt what we can become, what we can achieve, and what we can create. We even take a stoic view on things, planning for the worst case. Instead of motoring self-assuredly into brightly lighted futures, we go into neutral mode, where indecision and detachment rule the road.

This condition can be likened again to filling a car with bad petrol. When an engine knocks, it releases pollution into the environment in the form of nitrogen oxide and raw, unburned hydrocarbons. These two chemicals are poisonous gases that show up as yellowish-brown colors in a polluted sky. They can also cause respiratory problems like asthma and emphysema. A knocking is never a good thing. Keep your filters clean and fuel your mind with "good gas" only.

Another roadblock to our ability to think optimistically is that we grow up hearing the word "no" too often. Even though it is probably the one word that is universally understood around the globe, when improperly or overly used, it takes on a negative power of its own that prevents us from shifting our mindset.

The good news is we can change this. We can empower our minds and accomplish what we never thought we could. How? By becoming shifters—by talking back to our thoughts, by verbalizing the way we want things to be, by declaring our destinies—by using the language of *YES!*

Yes, a small but mighty word. During my previous consulting work with marketing agencies, one Creative Director had an interesting ritual for blue sky brainstorm sessions. Each participant was asked to wear a circular red sticker that said simply, "Yes." It was her way of reminding us to keep an open mind regarding far out ideas and to not immediately go to why the idea would NOT work. In other words, we were only to enter the brainstorm space with a YES mentality.

If you want to be a success, you have to get used to frequently hearing the word no and ignoring it. 98% of adults are conditioned to stop when they hear the word no. If you want to be in the top two percent, you have to get real. Do not let somebody's arbitrary no stop you. Find a creative way to sidestep the no. —Donald Trump

---

During his campaign, President Obama repeated the word *"yes"* a lot to subliminally train the thinking of supporters and to claim his victory. This small but powerful word also helped introduce his way of thinking to the world. "Yes I can" and "yes we can" became prophetic themes in his speeches and campaign collateral from day one all the way through to his acceptance speech. How can saying and thinking "yes" more help you shift your brilliance?

Maybe by now you are thinking, "Simon, I'm not the President of the United States, and you don't have a clue what it's like to be in my shoes." You know what? You're right! I don't know. My own life has been no bed of roses, yet I'm not even going to pretend that I understand what you may have faced—unimaginable pain, disappointment, and heartache.

But what I do know is that even those who have been dealt the cruelest of blows can see what's possible. How do I know this?

Because I personally know people who are living extraordinary lives despite broken marriages, broken hearts, broken dreams, broken promises, and just plain brokenness.

This is a known fact: Your life will move in the direction of your most dominant dialogue. For example, if your conversations are full of gloom and doom, if you are constantly talking about the recession, pending layoffs, the mortgage industry, or your depleted retirement account, you won't find your inner confidence.

If anyone understands the power of words, and if there is one who would be considered a master wordsmith, it is new age marketing genius Seth Godin. He is the author of the number one most read marketing blog on the World Wide Web and author of 17 national best-selling books translated into more than 35 languages. He is arguably one of the most respected marketing and advertising thought leaders of our time. The once Vice President of Direct Marketing at Yahoo! was recently inducted into the Direct Marketing Hall of Fame, one of only three professionals chosen for this honor. His mantras to "stand up and stand out, change everything, and never fit in" have dubbed him the rebel of status quo acting, thinking, and being. Recently turning the world of book publishing upside down by launching a series of four books via Kickstarter.com and reaching its campaign goal within an unprecedented three hours, I would definitely consider him the poster child of shifting his brilliance and Vujá dé thinking.

You will either rise or fall based on the words you put forth. If you say it, it becomes real, for better or for worse. If what you are experiencing right now is not in alignment with what you see in your mind's eye, then change your conversation.

For ideas and examples of the power of words, visit www. shiftyourbrilliance.com.

Simon T. Says... A negative attitude and outlook come as a result of what you are feeding into your system. If you listen to the news and associate with people who believe the sky is falling, then they will rub off on you. Strange, but true. So, here is what you can do about it: Speak positively. Every morning, take 15 minutes to get into the zone—five minutes to meditate, five minutes to read something that inspires you, and five minutes to exercise or stretch. When you do this, then you will experience an internal shift that will get you through the day. When you lose something, just say to yourself—I believe I will find something better.

It didn't take me long to realize that negativity, pessimism, and cynicism are contagious, and that you can either feed into another person's dismal outlook or you can walk the other way. A negative outlook has a viral effect that spreads from the mind to the lips, from the lips to the hands, and from the hands to the feet.

How to Create Contagious Optimism

Individuals who subscribe to the contagiously optimistic mind-set demonstrate the following behaviors:

- They see the tank half full when others see it half empty and they say so.

- They use positive language.

- They leave or stand up for the victims when people gossip about others.

- They ask the right questions to get everyone else in the room thinking and moving; they see themselves

as the match that gets the fire going; they see themselves as the solution.

- They know that organizations don't just employ,
  they deploy people to urge the rest of the company
  to rise to the occasion and seize the moment.

- They erase all negative thoughts.

- They recognize that both pessimism and optimism
  are as infectious as the flu and choose which to per-
  sonify; they embrace positive psychology as a way
  of life.

- They celebrate mistakes as well as accomplishments;
  they realize that people don't work in departments,
  they work in teams.

- They smile in their hearts, and it shows on their faces.

Choose Only High-Grade Relationships

There are generally three types of petrol for most traditional
vehicles (not counting the diesel-powered and hybrids out there).
They are: high octane, middle grade, or lower grade. The same
can be said for relationships with others. There are the high-octane
people who give us energy and encouragement, the middle-grade
ones who give us just enough power to keep us moving, and then
the lower-grade ones who hold us back from meeting our potential.

When you are trying to decide whether a relationship fuels
your mind, take note of how others speak to you. Are their words
uplifting or crippling? If they're positive and supportive, you will
be reenergized. If they're negative and hurtful, your energy will be
quickly drained.

Is it perhaps time for you to take back your life and stop letting negative people deplete your energy reserves? Is this your shift opportunity? Do yourself a favor and empty your tank of those who zap your energy.

Simon T. Says... If you want to know your future, look at the people in your life. Do they stretch you? If not shift!

Beware the Backseat Drivers

Have you ever been driving down the road and someone else in your car keeps correcting you, telling you where to go, or worse yet, are dash grabbers? High-octane relationships don't include these backseat drivers—the naysayers or control freaks in our lives. But, inevitably in business situations, we will encounter negative, backseat drivers. Here's my story on this topic.

I recently submitted one of my how-to success guides to an international company for distribution. A few weeks later, a Dear John letter arrived in my mailbox: "After careful review of the information submitted, it has been decided that our distribution enterprise will *not* be accepting your success guide." The correspondence closed with, "All the best wishes for your success!"

I take rejections as someone blowing a bugle
in my ear to wake me up and get going, rather
than retreat. —Sylvester Stallone, actor

That letter arrived not long after I had received a rejection e-mail from another major distributor. It said in part, "Simon, we will not pursue carrying your success book. It is not strong enough. Thank you for sharing it with us. Continued success!"

Continued success? How encouraging is *that?*

In the past, I would have looked at these responses and crumbled. I might have even given up and thought, "All that work down the drain!" But I'm older now—and I've been to Paris! I've chalked up a few experiences that have taught me how to cope with disappointment. So instead, I answered the e-mail rejection with an e-mail of my own. "This is brilliant news," I wrote. "I am so excited! Wow! Stay Brilliant…Simon T. Bailey."

No, I wasn't trying to be sarcastic. I was being sincere. See, I have learned to shift and to celebrate rejection. I have learned to take the energy of rejection and experience a shift in my brilliance. I reframe it and see it as a gift, a blessing in disguise. My rejecters have done me a favor; they have saved me time, energy, and money. Most importantly, I have been given an invitation to grow.

So what happened to change my perspective? How can I be so positive and passionate about being rejected? Well, there are a number of reasons, but mostly it is because I believe in my own worth, choose high-octane relationships, and see my tank as half full.

What I've discovered is that every rejection is one step closer to an acceptance. I ended up self-publishing my success guide titled *Release Your Brilliance* over six years ago. Since then, I've presented it to numerous agents, publishers, and distributors, and I've experienced mostly rejection.

But do you know what I found out? It only takes one—one person or one organization to catch the vision. I was actually blessed to find two—my agent Dupree/Miller & Associates and my editor at HarperCollins Business Publishing. Both of them understood and saw the value in what I had to say. I am honored to be able to tell you that a hardcover edition of *Release Your Brilliance* was finally published.

So every time my book was rejected, I knew I was that much closer to finding "the one" who would accept it. Several corporate clients have ordered thousands of copies of *Release Your Brilliance*, and at a recent convention for an international organization where I spoke on the topic of success, the bookstore sold out of it. I'm very proud, and share this with you only as an example of my rejection theory working at its best.

Incidentally, *Zen and the Art of Motorcycle Maintenance: An Inquiry into Values*, which I referenced earlier, sold over four million copies in 27 languages and was described by the press as the "most widely read philosophy book." And, according to the *Guinness World Records*, 121 publishers originally rejected it, more than any other best-selling book!

I'm asking you to shift your ideas about rejection and do the following:

- Dare to be rejected!
- Own your rejection and reframe it!
- Look for creative ways to sidestep the *no*'s and realize they are but invitations to grow.

Now, when I put myself out there, I think: "Reject me, Baby! Tell me *no*. Cast me off and kick me to the curb. I relish it!" In the immortal words of the Terminator, "I'll be back."

What about you? When you inevitably experience rejection, will you be defeated? Will you become stuck in a neutral gear, or worse yet, reverse?

Or will you get up, dust yourself off, and keep on going?

I realize that you may have also had to deal with rejection—for things more drastic than being refused by a publisher. In fact, like me, you may have an advanced degree in the subject of Rejection.

You may feel as if you've been cast out, written off, and thrown away. Things haven't worked out the way you expected and wanted. You're rightfully discouraged because you've been spurned so often.

Understand that not everyone is going to appreciate you. There will be many people—too many people—who won't see or recognize your brilliance. There will be people who will reject your genius and overlook your potential. There will be people who will not accept your love or your wisdom. Many will tell you *no*. So what you must do is get those *no*'s out of the way and find your one *yes*!

Expand Your Network

Networking is essential for both new jobs and business contacts and a great way to fuel your mind. In fact, research says that effective networking is 12 times more potent than answering advertisements. An indirect approach is better than a direct one. It's a way to find hidden opportunities and can set you apart from the competition.

If you need to find a job or shift from the one you are in, connect with others in your field. Sign up for LinkedIn, Facebook, or Meetup. The new capital in the 21st century is the people who will promote your brand when you are not around.

If you are currently employed, build a network of partners to keep an open eye and ear for new opportunities that might suit you. Make a point once a week to go to lunch with different people in different departments. For a 45 minute lunch, have three questions to prime the conversation pump. The first should be personally related (to create a common ground and break down any barriers). The second question should be business related, and the third future related, creating an opportunity to find out how you can fuel each other's objectives.

I recently received a note from Ryan, a Sales Executive for a home health services company, about the power of expanding his network. He shifted his brilliance by trying something he'd never previously thought of to increase sales. He networked to build a partnership with the director of a local residential rehab center's council on aging. The center had tight ties in the local community and also had a small clinic run by one of Ryan's physicians a few days a week. Through this partnership, Ryan was able to gain access to a physician with whom he normally would not have had a way to connect. He took it a step further and also agreed to help introduce the director to his accounts in the community, so that the rehab centers could also increase business. This type of reciprocity is a key ingredient in successfully expanding your network.

If you are looking for companionship, consider community centers, singles associations, and local gathering places—the safe ones, of course! There are a lot of single people out there waiting for Mr. or Ms. Right, believing that when he or she appears, life will be wonderful. But when you believe you need something, that's exactly where you will stay—in need. Instead, decide right now to find people not just for what you can receive from them, but for how you can fuel each other. Invest your time and energy in these people.

Tear down the walls you've built to keep others out. Ask God to send help, and then open your eyes, your ears, and your heart so you will recognize it when it arrives. When you help yourself, other people will show up to assist you.

Networking Tips

- Get into the habit of being talkative. Have a line ready!
- Talk to everyone you know about opportunities.

- Find those friendly network spiders, those types of people who just seem to know everyone. Go out of your way to be where people are. Introduce yourself to everyone.

- Get the contact details of people you meet; exchange business cards.

- Go to every social gathering you are invited to. Make connections and find common interests.

- Be willing and able to talk about your achievements. (But don't brag!)

- Reach out to people with whom you've lost contact.

Maybe your opportunity to shift is simply to get out and meet just one person. Perhaps you spend too much time alone. While alone time can be healthy because it allows for introspection and meditation, feeling lonely doesn't fuel your mind. Being alone is a state of being physically separated from other people. Few of us on the planet are truly alone. However, millions of us are lonely, lacking companionship and human touch. Loneliness, though, is a temporary state, one that you can change. How? Choose to leave loneliness behind.

What are you waiting for?

Simon T. Says... If you want to grow your business, connect first, sell last.

Find a Mentor

Probably one of the highest-octane relationships you can engage in is that with a mentor. Unlike the more-often-than-not downbeat backseat driver, a mentor serves as a positive copilot, guiding you along your journey.

For you to release your brilliance in all the facets of your life, you will need a mentor, which I often refer to as a "brilliandeer." A brilliandeer is a highly-skilled craftsperson whose sole responsibility is to shape and polish a diamond during its transformation from rough stone to a brilliant, shining gem. Do you have a brilliandeer who is helping you smooth the rough edges and polish the facets of your brilliance?

Mentors have an uncanny ability to teach, model, and illuminate darkness through their shining light of intelligence. They challenge you to be different. How so? They think differently, act differently, and respond differently to many of the same circumstances you encounter. They Vujá dé. True mentors are nonconformists who march to the beat of a different drummer, yet they refrain from making you just like they are. Their purpose in your life is to serve as a guide for you, but not to decide for you. They can lead you to water, but they cannot make you drink.

You will need brilliandeers/mentors all your life, but especially from age 18 to 35, which psychologist Daniel Levinson calls the "life structure era." Once you reach age 36, then you are in a position to be a brilliandeer to others. This is one of my desires—to be a mentor and help others release and shift their brilliance.

I have been on a journey for the past 20 years to live my purpose to the utmost. I have struggled, cried, and laughed with the best of them, and I have also often crawled back into my hole, wishing someone would tell me what to do. At the critical junctures of my journey, there were always mentors who helped shape my diamond brilliance. Meet my brilliandeers and discover what each of them taught me.

Mentor	Valuable Lesson
My parents	The way up is down. In other words, always be grateful and humble for everything.
Mark Chironna	Increase your self-worth instead of your net worth.
Joel Novak	Institutionalize the brilliance methodology.
Patricia Engfer	Always help others when you can.
Carolyn Fennell	Articulate carefully and communicate with ease and comfort.
Ralph Veerman	Give of your time, talent, and resources without expecting anything in return.
Larry Krieder	Character and integrity are two of the most important qualities of a good man.
Jerry Wilson	Stay spiritually fit at all times.

Ask yourself:

- Who is my mentor—who is shaping me?

- Who is helping me shift out of neutral?

- Who is helping me Vujá dé?

- Am I relying on a friend, who, like me, is struggling to find his or her place, purpose, and position in life?

- Or is my mentor a true brilliandeer who possesses a cornucopia of knowledge born of experience that can be critical to helping me find the combination to the vault where my diamond potential is kept?

Today, thank the mentors who are shaping you into a brilliant gemstone. Appreciate them and love them for being interested and concerned about your development. And if you don't have a brilliandeer, decide which areas of your life need the most attention.

Then, ask around to see who might be a good fit as a mentor for you. Remember, when the student is ready, the teacher will appear.

A diligent mentor will expose attempts at excuse-
making and will help you uncover and dispel any
unspoken fears or self-limiting attitudes and behaviors.
—Mark Chironna, author of *Live Your Dream*

Become a Lifelong Learner

Another way to fuel your mind is to keep your intellectual tank full. In other words, keep your brain running on all cylinders! Do you read regularly? Just like we tell our children, it doesn't matter if it's fiction, motivational, or hobby-related as long as you are reading to increase your knowledge and challenge your mind.

Most likely, you will shift several times in your life. To be ready, have your mental gears engaged. Commit to being a lifelong learner. Just like when you're taking a long journey, you can't look at MapQuest or your directions only once and know the way.

Are you current in your field? Up to date on market and industry trends? Tuned in to the latest advice on making families and relationships work? Up to par on your skill set?

If you didn't answer yes to all of the above, get current, brush up, and do it quickly. Take some night courses at your local college or attend a professional development seminar. With technology at our fingertips, there are online courses you can take advantage of—some are even free. You can sign up for online tutorials on computer software skills through certain vendors such as Microsoft.

As the U.S. Bureau of Labor and Statistics (BLS) reports, the amount of education an individual obtains has a major impact on that person's earning potential. BLS states that individuals with only a high school diploma earned on average $626 a week in 2009 and those with a Bachelor's degree earned $1,025 a week during the same year. Those who hold graduate degrees earn even more, according to these statistics, indicating a direct correlation between the money spent on education and the money you earn.

Take some classes, pursue an advanced degree, study a new field—become an expert at something.

If you are in the job market, learn everything you can about the company with which you are interviewing. What are their values? What are their core products? Who is their primary competition? What's their annual revenue? Most of this information is available publicly.

Subscribe to online business resources like FastCompany.com, Wired.com, TheOptimist.com, and Economist.com, to name just a few. Check out the following blogs, Internet news wires, and educational sites: DanielPink.com, SethGodin.com, HuffingtonPost.com, TheDailyBeast.com, PopTech.com, and Ted.com.

And if you are currently in a job, do the same thing! Learn everything there is to know about your current company. Read the annual reports. Study the company's culture, history, and success stories. Cross-pollinate by finding out what's happening in other departments and what value you can bring to them. Understanding what makes the organization tick, discovering the unspoken do's and don'ts, and identifying what works and what doesn't will allow you to effectively position yourself without hindering your career.

Scan the Internet regularly for blogs and other press pieces. Is your company in the news? Why? Are they still creating products and a presence that make you proud to represent them? If so, are you doing your part? Are you upholding the brand? Even if you are not in the job of your dreams, it is your responsibility to be loyal and productive for the time being. You're still getting a paycheck, right? And remember, how you conduct yourself in your current position sets the tone and foundation for the next one.

I am learning all the time. The tombstone
will be my diploma. —Eartha Kitt

One of my clients recently shared with me her frustration with her assistant. She had asked her to do what she thought was a simple task in Microsoft Outlook, and her assistant couldn't do it. My client said, "You've been here for 21 years, so you should know how to do it." The assistant replied, "You are the first person who has asked me to think in seven years."

In an era of significant global competition with the BRICS nations (Brazil, Russia, India, China, and South Africa), there is no room for being an anemic thinker. In a decade-long study by McKinsey & Company, the total market capitalization of the largest 150 companies grew 11% per year. However, the top 30 companies experienced a 22% increase in market capitalization and net income. What drove the results for the top 30 was the value of thinking-intensive workers. These are men and women who found a way to expand their knowledge bandwidth and thought differently about their work. They approached it as a career to build instead of a job to have.

A thinking-intensive individual is a shifter—constantly scanning the environment to see where things are headed. Shifters have a knack for reading the tea leaves of the times and thinking like a poker strategist. People who don't think become robotic in their execution. People who do think ask, "Why are we doing this?" and "Is there a better way?" People who don't think are waiting to be told what to do. People who do think make it happen.

According to the U.S. Census Bureau, 97% of business revenue is controlled by 16% of business owners. That leaves the other 84% of business owners to chase the 3% that is leftover business revenue. Why such a disparity? The 16% think differently.

What about you? Do you shift your brilliance often? Do you think differently? Do you see the future in the present, or do you see what everyone else sees and accept it at face value? If you are in the 84% mentioned above, fuel your mind and look to your destination. Everything we are witnessing in the world—the Egyptian revolt, Libya's $70 billion in hidden wealth, and Zimbabwe's controversies—point to men and women fed up with someone else doing the thinking for them. Thanks to the Internet, these oppressed men and women have seen the benefits of a liberated mindset with which people are free to think beyond daily survival. Though the initial quest for ultimate freedom may escape their grasp, it will forever be imprinted on the canvas of their minds. Today, make the shift. Let go of what you know and be open to receiving that which you don't know.

---

*Simon T. Says...*Crack open the door of your mind and let in a fresh wind of possibilities.

Shift Your Brilliance Moment: I recommend that you read the list of books outlined at the end of this book.

TAKE THE WHEEL

To change what's outside, look inside to see who's at the wheel. You hold the keys to your destiny! You're in control of the car. So, go ahead and accept that awesome responsibility and take the wheel. As I've said earlier in the book, instead of letting tomorrow come to you, go to it. Own your future! Don't let fear of failure and the changes that are happening at full speed around you keep you in neutral. Go ahead and shift! Believe me, there is no better time to become a shifter than now. With unemployment at about 10% and job layoffs at a record high, this is no time to say, "It's not my job," or "They didn't hire me to do that."

> The future is not a result of choices among alternative paths offered by the present, but a place that is created—created first in the mind and will, created next in activity. The future is not some place we are going to, but one we are creating. —Unknown

How committed are you to keeping your promises, fulfilling your vision, and making the changes that are necessary to shift? Are you taking complete ownership of your destiny?

Ultimately, taking the wheel is about ownership. You are the operator of the vehicle that is your life. In fact, while there may be others along the way who offer encouragement and support, you are the only one who owns your future and the only one who can determine the next step on your journey.

Before you take the wheel:

- Check Your Balance and Alignment

- Recalibrate Your Internal GPS

- Don't Be Afraid to Make a U-Turn

- Fail Faster (yes, I know it sounds strange, but trust me...)

Check Your Balance and Alignment

An important part of taking control of your vehicle is to check your balance. If your wheels are out of balance, you're in for a bumpy ride. It's the same in life, if certain aspects of it are out of balance.

Balance comes in part from living a simplified life. Does that surprise you? Perhaps you thought that taking control to meet demands more effectively would require multitasking. But not so. Research confirms that multitasking actually makes you less efficient, not more.

Multitaskers, whose full attention is not devoted to the task at hand, often don't take the time to fully understand the breadth and depth of a project. Because of that, they get only mediocre results.

> When you do two things at once, brain power doesn't
> increase to meet the demand. In fact it decreases
> which means you perform each task more poorly than
> if you focused on one alone. —Edward Willett

Creating balance in your life is a continuous process. And it's not an easy task. Demands on your time change as family, interests, and work requirements change. Assess your situation every few months to make sure you're staying on track. And by the way, balance doesn't mean doing everything. Re-examine your priorities and set boundaries. Be honest with yourself in what you can and cannot do. Only you can restore harmony to your lifestyle, and this often requires a shift.

A quick win is streamlining and simplifying. De-clutter your world by employing the OHIO rule as much as possible: Only Handle It Once! A clean desk doesn't necessarily equate to more productive work, but there's no question that a cluttered area that silently asks you, "Where are you going to begin?" will severely dampen your enthusiasm for giving extra effort. The following are a few tips.

Tips to Streamline and Simplify

- Eliminate that pile of papers on your desk.
- Anything more than six months old is irrelevant—the world has changed.
- If the item doesn't relate to something that drives revenue or reduces expenses, trash it.
- Ask yourself, "What's the worst that can happen if I don't take action on this item?"

- Clean out your filing cabinet.

- Go through and organize your papers and folders.

- Schedule time to purge your files. This can be done monthly, quarterly, biannually or even annually; just make sure you do it on a regular basis.

- Demystify complex tasks and projects by breaking them down into bite-size chunks and then focusing clearly on each chunk. Doing so allows you to attend to the details that drive exceptional and unexpected results.

- Write things down! Better yet, Yellow Pages taught us years ago to let our fingers do the walking. Leverage the tools on your personal digital assistant, e-tablet, or laptop. This will save time and frustration later. Why take the chance of forgetting an appointment when it only takes seconds to write it down?

- Schedule block times to work on similar tasks.

- Pay bills and enter the items in your money management program while everything is on your desk and fresh in your mind.

- Make all your phone calls in one sitting.

- Sign birthday, holiday, and business cards for the whole month in one sitting.

Recalibrate Your Internal GPS

We've got not only road signs, traffic lights, city maps, mile markers, street names, roadside assistance services, and MapQuest, we've also got our built-in global positioning system (GPS). I don't know about you, but when I'm motoring along and I don't know where I'm going, I place my full and complete trust in the Australian male voice on my GPS. Even so, there are times when he starts commanding me to turn when there's no turn, make a left when there's no left, or keep going straight when there's a dead end. These times are rare, but when it happens, I start improvising, he keeps correcting, and then he starts recalibrating. That's when I know my GPS has lost its way, needs time to take a cyber-breath, and start over.

This happens in real life, too. Sometimes we think we are ready to shift, but we might be misinformed or momentarily lost. It's then that we need to recalibrate.

After I left the Disney Corporation and started my own business, I began hearing voices. Really, it's true. But I wasn't going crazy. (While I am perhaps over the top as far as energy and enthusiasm go, I know I'm not totally bonkers.) I was just coming under the powerful spell of negative thinking.

> If you want to soar into a new dimension, then
> let go of what is comfortable and expand your
> wings of possibility. —Simon T. Bailey

Throughout the day, I would hear, "You should have stayed at that job; you should have structured your company differently; you should have hired a president and CEO while you worked on the creative side. You should have done this, you should have done that."

With my head in my arms and my hands over my ears one day, sick of the racket those gremlins of confidence were making inside of my mind, I realized I had to shift my energy. I got very quiet and I told them I wouldn't accept what they had to say. I deleted them; I erased their harmful internal chatter. I had to, or they would have eaten me alive.

Okay, I realize I've made it sound easy, wiping out those adverse thoughts. Just do it, right? Just stop that stinking thinking! But the truth is, it was anything but easy. I worked hard to will myself into being a positive, confident person. I practiced and practiced articulating the future I wanted to live in until I was blue in the face. I had to recalibrate my internal GPS. I had to Vujá dé my outlook.

Recalibrating your internal compass gives you a new way to look at things and erases erroneous beliefs about what you have or haven't done. It helps you live the future now. Sometimes you simply have to press reset and start fresh. Hitting reset can realign your heart, your mind, and your spirit with your plan and your goals. Hitting reset gets you unstuck, gets you out of neutral and functioning once again. Hitting reset allows you to emerge as the person you were made to be.

Not long ago, I'd been having problems with my cell phone—it just hadn't been working quite right. I called the service line, and the representative suggested I push the phone's reset button to restore the settings to their original programming. Realizing I had nothing to lose except some reprogramming time, I did it—and it was like having a brand-new phone! All the issues were swept away, the erroneous programming wiped clean. My phone and I had a fresh start.

Don't Be Afraid to Make a U-Turn

Sometimes, when you're trying to follow the advice of your GPS (even when it is correct) or the coordinates of your map, you might still make a mistake and need to turn around.

Making a U-turn has gotten a bad name. In some instances, it's illegal to make a U-turn, and signs are posted warning us of this. In other cases, making a U-turn might in fact be legal, but there is the danger of getting stuck in the middle or having to enter fast-moving, oncoming traffic.

Sometimes seeing differently requires that we make U-turns. After all, Vujá dé is déjà vu making a U-turn! When we have missed our turn or made a wrong choice, turning around and going in the opposite direction may be our only option. Life is like this too. If we get passed over for an opportunity or make a wrong choice, then we have to choose a different path.

Let's face it, if you are a typical male like I am, you don't like to take directions from anyone, especially your spouse. You know how it goes—you're driving down the road with your significant other, or you're talking or listening to the radio. You miss your turn and end up driving 30 minutes in the wrong direction. When this happens to me, my wife of 17 years looks at me with "those eyes" that say, "I told you so," and oh, so much more. So, then you do it—you make the necessary U-turn that signifies your error. You turn around, and now you are on your way in the right direction.

Although a U-turn typically implies "do over" or an "error," I know people who have gotten their personal lives together despite huge impediments because they weren't afraid to make sweeping changes in their lives. Take my friend Stewart.

Stewart's Story

Stewart left a Fortune 100 company to go work with a technology company. The perks and the benefits package of the new job were unbelievable. In fact, if the company were to have gone public, Stewart would've been able to exercise his lucrative stock options and make enough money to feed a small nation.

After a few months at the job, Stewart was driving to work one day when he completely broke down. Mind you, my friend is fifty years old, a meat-and-potatoes kind of guy, a man's man. And there he was, sobbing like a newborn baby on his way to his crème de la crème job. I asked him why this happened, and he said, "It was at that moment when I realized I was only going through the motions at work. I was just doing a job. I'd lost my passion."

Here he was enjoying a happy marriage with beautiful children, living in a lovely home with a vacation house to escape to on the weekends, and keeping plenty of money in the bank—you know, everyone's ultimate dream. Yet there was a hole in his soul. He'd gained weight, lost what little hair he had, and was generally stressed out. Work had become nothing more than a place to show up and collect a check. Stewart had...

- Success but no significance,
- Money but no meaning,
- Power but no purpose, and
- Status but no satisfaction.

He was alive in body but dead in spirit. And that's precisely when he knew it was time to shift. After a few months of soul (and job) searching, he launched a new company with a group of partners and has absolutely found his niche. Stewart feels alive again—he's lost weight, let go of the stress, and according to his doctor, has the heart of a 35-year-old man. He's in the best shape of his life and happier than he's ever been.

Think about how often in life we continue to head in one direction, even if it's the wrong one, because it's all we've known. How many people do you know who show up for work every Monday morning to a job they dread and co-workers they dislike? The reality is that sometimes you have to make a U-turn, because the direction you're heading is not where you want to go. That's exactly what my friend Stewart had the courage to do.

Following are some signs that it's time to make a U-turn. Check the ones that apply to your situation. If you select more than one, it's time to turn.

Tell-Tale Signs It's Time to Make a U-Turn

- Your zest for adventure is gone, and you don't know where it went.

- You've started a project several times, but for some reason, you just can't bring yourself to finish it.

- You've been working on creating a business, and it seems as if you start and stop, start and stop.

- You're in a dead-end relationship with no energy, no fun, no mutual respect. You're always the one giving and never receiving.

- You're in a job that gives you no sense of purpose, no intellectual stimulation.

- You dread going home.

- You dread leaving home.

- You interact with an association you are now ashamed to be part of.

- You're driving to work or school or where you go every day, and you are tempted to deliberately pass your exit.

- Your environment lacks energy, peace, or fun.

- Your employer has laid off a lot of workers, and now you are doing the job of five to seven people.

- You have a sense in your gut, or you hear that little voice in your head that says, "This is not working for me anymore."

- Your job is just a job. There is no fulfillment, no satisfaction; you're just running on the treadmill. The only reason you're still there is because you need the money.

- You show up physically at work (even if you have a home office), but your mind drifts throughout the day, and you wonder what else you could be doing.

- The economy has perhaps knocked the wind out of your sails, and you need a new perspective.

Simon T. Says... Shift or be shifted!

Fail Faster

William Lazarus, President and CEO of Seer Analytics, LLC, made a powerful statement during a Tampa CEO Council meeting where I was privileged to speak. He said all his employees know that the company mantra in times past was "Make new mistakes!" This year it's "Make mistakes faster!" The rationale behind this thinking is that if you are making mistakes early and often, then in the long run your cost of entry into a new marketplace decreases, and sustaining market share becomes easier because you fail forward.

Another CEO, who shall remain nameless, stated that what burns him are employees who are trained, coached, and retold a million times how to do a specific job and still don't get it right. They trip over themselves, always wanting to get face time with him or anyone on his senior team, but they do not pay attention to the work at hand. He looked around the table hoping his fellow CEOs could offer solutions, but many just nodded their heads in empathy because they could relate to his pain.

Corporations don't have ideas—thinking people do. If organizations are to continue to thrive, an internal group of men and women must exist who are given the autonomy to create the future. They must be fully funded and given the chance to fail forward. They are not handcuffed to corporate legacy, but unleashed to make brilliant shifts toward what the company will be in the future.

If your organization is to create the future now, then what bold steps will you take to fail on purpose? There are lessons for leaders and teams to learn on the road to brilliance.

For an individual, failing faster is taking one step toward the direction of resistance. In Steven Pressfield's book, *The War of Art—Winning the Inner Creative Battle,* he says:

> Like a magnetized needle floating on a surface of oil, Resistance will unfailingly point to true North—meaning that calling or action it most wants to stop us from doing. The more important a call or action is to our soul's evolution the more Resistance we will feel toward pursuing it.

ENGAGE YOUR GEARS

By now, you have given your Vujá dé a chance. You have adopted a new way of seeing things, harnessed your inner strength, ignited your passion, fueled your mind, and taken the wheel. It's time now to engage those gears! Sometimes, though, when we attempt to shift, we can either grind a gear or slip out of a gear. When this happens, it's important to remember that making changes in our lives is often challenging. For a new behavior to become a habit, it must be reinforced at least 17 to 21 times. Making lasting changes requires commitment, persistence, and discipline.

So the last step before you actually restart your internal engine is to consider what will give you the energy and the discipline to get in gear and *stay* in gear. Furthermore, in your business, what will you do to implement Vujá dé into your daily routine?

To engage your gears, to shift yourself and your team, and to create the future now, consider how and when to:

- Buckle Down

- Maximize Your Energy
- Drive Value

Buckle Down

When you get in your car, or someone else's for that matter, what is the first thing you do? You put on your seat belt, right? You buckle up to protect yourself along the journey. To shift, you want to buckle down—that is, find the self-discipline to safe-guard your progress.

Carissa and Bob's Story

One of my favorite couples, Carissa and Bob, sent me an update regarding the progress of their budding cupcake business, which reminded me of the vital lesson that inevitably comes after you shift your brilliance—to buckle down. On the couple's behalf, Carissa wrote:

> Honestly, most people really don't want to hear how hard the last two years have been. When you asked us to write about how we were inspired to shift our brilliance, I can honestly say it was through blood, sweat, tears, and desperation that grew into inspiration…pain that grew into passion. When we didn't have another option, we submitted to the only option at hand. We searched deep within ourselves and relied on our faith in God.
>
> I don't believe we would have ever taken the risk (or leap of faith) if we had had any other options (LOL). When we no longer had a weekly salary, and no doors opening for a "regular" job, we turned to what was in our hand, our hobby, and used it to launch a full-time business. We went from door to door selling our cupcakes and had to

make a living, $3 at a time. We used to tease one another when we would consider buying something, and say, "Now, that's 20 cupcakes. Do we really need it?"

We realize now when we look back at the path, it was all directed by God, and each stepping stone was a learning and growing time. But it did not come easy. We still do not feel we have "arrived" and we're still growing in our skill and craft, as well as growing our business. But we do feel confident in knowing we are fulfilling our purpose and passion and God has been there, every step of the way.

We've been working in the market place for two years now, and we realize the influence we can potentially have and the people we can potentially reach through this business. The example we can be in the community is a great responsibility, and we do not take lightly. We just let our lives reflect who we are and who He is to us.

Thank you for making a difference in our lives...for encouraging us. When others saw a failure, you saw our brilliance.

The seatbelt is necessary, because it won't always be easy; problems will arise, but we have to continually look for new perspectives and be determined to see things differently with the expectation of brilliant outcomes.

Shift Your Thinking

"We cannot solve our problems with the same thinking we used to create them." That sage perspective comes from the father of modern physics, Albert Einstein.

Companies and entrepreneurs are shifting their brilliance to differentiate themselves in the marketplace as well as generate great results for their immediate customers and beyond.

Do you remember when water was free? I sure do. Just when the country was getting used to paying for bottled water, the beverage industry had a Vujá dé moment and introduced the same water in a new way. One remarkable example of a shift in traditional thinking is the growing and profitable "enhanced water" market.

Before brokering a multi-billion dollar deal with the Coca-Cola Company, Glaceau, the maker of Vitaminwater, was your typical upstart beverage company working hard to expand its consumer base beyond New York. Glaceau Marketing Executive Rohan Oza, who calls himself a "brand Messiah," stayed in a perpetual state of shifting in those early days by first abandoning traditional marketing methods to instead send a fleet of taste-testing vehicles staffed by "hydrologists" all across the nation, then later bartering the deal with entertainer 50 Cent to help promote the brand (against the advisement of stakeholders), and eventually going back to his previous employer, Coca-Cola, to help mediate the acquisition of the brand by the mega company.

No one, and I mean no one, wants to be the face behind a boring, lifeless presentation, right? Well, as a result of Vujá dé thinking, a pair of junior Louisiana State University students decided they had seen their last drab, 200-page PowerPoint presented by a Fortune 500 executive or recruiter brought on campus to inspire or impress them. The two started a business called Big Fish Presentations, focused on creating engaging, tech-savvy, and creative presentation content for companies looking to improve their recruiting, new-hire training, or new business presentations. They shifted their brilliance to look for new ways to solve an old problem. To their surprise, they were invited to appear on ABC's show "Shark Tank." Although they declined, the company continues to experience record growth. Not bad for two entrepreneurs still sharing a dorm room.

Here are five ways to implement a little shift of brilliance in your organization:

- *Go where the answers are.* Front-line is the Bottom Line. The answers you need are not at the top of the food chain; they are at the bottom of the food chain. They exist in the heads, hearts, and hands of the men and women who are closest to your customers. Ask front-line employees what clients are asking for that currently may not be offered. You may be surprised by some of their answers.

- *Use synergy as green energy.* What creative breakthroughs are your third-party vendors introducing that may offer a competitive edge for you? How might they be customized for your organization? When was the last time you shared your strategic vision with them or asked them how you might collectively reach the customers you share?

- *Fight the gravitational pull in the marketplace to be average.* Challenge colleagues to come up with breakthrough suggestions that take everything you do to the next level. Visit Ideastring.com and use its software system to harness the brilliance within your organization. Stop accepting mediocre thinking. Fear and complacency keep many organizations stuck in neutral. Shift gears by pushing the envelope and asking, "Where's the Vujá dé?"

- *Take your core team on a field trip to other industries.* See what they do well and how they implement creativity into their culture. Then invite your core leaders to make a presentation about what they learned and how they intend to use it in their organization.

- *Become your customer.* Shop your experience. What would you do differently after experiencing how you treat the new customers and members that you want to attract?

Maximize Your Energy

How do you know when to *preserve* versus *expend* your energy? Remember your core motivator? The first order of business is to direct all your energy toward that. Leverage your knowledge of what drives you to get the juices flowing.

There is a movement in the United States to conserve fuel in response to astronomical gas prices...more than $4 per gallon in certain parts of the country. (You may remember when gas was under $1 per gallon!) Just as there are many ways to save physical energy like fossil fuels, you can also maximize your personal energy—the source of your personal power.

The word "energy" first appeared in 1599 and represents *power*. So when you conserve your energy, you really are conserving your personal power. Conversely, if you're over-expending your energy in a dead-end relationship, job, or situation that drains you instead of recharges you, you're wasting your personal power. The trick with personal energy, like any kind of required resource, is to use it wisely.

Over the years, I've observed many people who waste their power source on minor issues, draining their energy to the point that they have none left when major opportunities present themselves. As a result, the brilliant opportunities of life often pass them by. This is how people become stuck in ruts. They become so mentally and spiritually exhausted that there's no energy left in their reserves.

One of the best ways to maximize your energy is to be selective about how and where you dispense it. Energy spent on the wrong activities is wasted energy, and the result is reduced productivity. However, energy invested in the right activities—those that really matter—drive the results and outcomes you want. Furthermore, targeted energy keeps you from multitasking your life away to accommodate all the competing agendas that want a piece of your time.

Here is a tool to evaluate how you are spending your time. Notice the difference between wasted and targeted energy. How well are you conserving YOUR fuel?

Occupation	Wasted Energy	Targeted Energy
Sales Professional	Cold calling	Leveraging existing relationships for referrals
Manager	Verbally abusing direct reports when they make a mistake	Asking direct reports what they learned as a result of their mistakes
Student	Lying to parents	Putting truth on the table and taking responsibility
Healthcare Executive	Telling employees they need to provide better service to patients	Providing better service for employees and then showing them how to better serve patients
You	Watching three to five hours of television	Reading, writing, journaling, or reflecting on life

Shift Your Brilliance Action Plan

Consider all the responsibilities that come with your job, business, or daily duties. Which ones energize you? Which ones do you avoid because you dislike them? Categorize your tasks and activities according to whether you consider them "Status quo" activities or "Brilliant Shift" activities, and then describe the "So WHAT?"

Status quo	Brilliant Shift	So WHAT?
Activities that take you off focus and deplete your energy.	Activities that keep you on target, give you energy, and move you toward what you love to do.	

Your energy is your very essence. When you conserve it and target it toward the right activities, you pull the future toward you instead of having to chase after it. What can you do to eliminate "status quo" activities or at least make them more energizing?

A Brilliant Shift

I was doing a presentation for 175 leaders and owners of the National Pest Control Management Association and asked them to complete the preceding exercise. The results were amazing. One of the big ideas of the day in their industry was this: Instead of sending out a man to engage a new homeowner in using their services, what if they sent out a woman to establish a rapport with the homeowner? They realized that most of the homeowner decisions are made by women, so having a female communicate with her made a positive difference to these companies.

Following are a few tips for conserving or replenishing your energy.

Tips for Maximizing Your Energy

- At your place of business, find a quiet spot where you can enjoy a 15- to 30- minute siesta every day. Or take a power walk! This is a good way to recharge your batteries, regain your focus, and reignite your brilliance.

- Volunteer in a meal kitchen or homeless shelter. These acts of kindness will so influence how you view the world that you will become reenergized from the inside out.

- Determine your "rhythm"—those times when you're most alert and "in the zone." Then, work on your difficult assignments during those productive times. Why? This is when things come most easily for you and when your inner drive for personal accountability is most alive.

- Work on tasks with a friend or colleague, or delegate them to someone who enjoys or has a talent for those tasks.

- Choose your battles carefully. Conserve your strength and save your ammunition for those fights you know you can win.

For more tips, visit www.shiftyourbrilliance.com.

Most people spend their entire lives in unquestionable routines, never hearing the calling of how great they could be if only they refocused on making a profound difference through their work.

—Roxanne Emmerich, author of *Thank God It's Monday*

Drive Value

When you're ready to pull forward, how do you know when to accelerate?

At the Brilliance Institute, we emphasize the importance of exceeding expectations. No matter what you are responsible for in life, accelerate your actions above and beyond what is expected or required. In other words, show some "drive." Meeting expectations simply isn't enough anymore. If you're only doing what is required, are you doing your best? Not likely. Doing the bare minimum translates to average, mediocre—just like everyone else. Bare minimum is weak.

Those who achieve great things push themselves to go the extra mile. Not because they have to or because someone makes them, but because they want to. If you're currently employed, for example, you're responsible for producing work that matters. The leadership of your organization doesn't have time to look over your shoulder to see if you're focusing on the right activities consistently, using the company's time wisely, and spending the company's resources prudently. When you were hired, you, in effect, agreed to an unwritten contract that you would take personal responsibility for your actions and represent the organization at all times in a positive light. How are you doing so far in this regard?

If you're concerned about the stability of your future, then drive value for your organization, your team, and your position, and you'll almost guarantee your continued employment, even in uncertain economic times.

Each moment of each day, you have the choice to go beyond your potential. Are you taking the initiative? Can you push yourself more? Use the following tool to determine how to accelerate your productivity levels.

Park, Start, or Accelerate: Driving Value Strategies

Write down which behaviors you need to put in park and which behaviors you need to start. What should you get even better at, or accelerate, in order to Vujá dé? Then share these with an accountability partner.

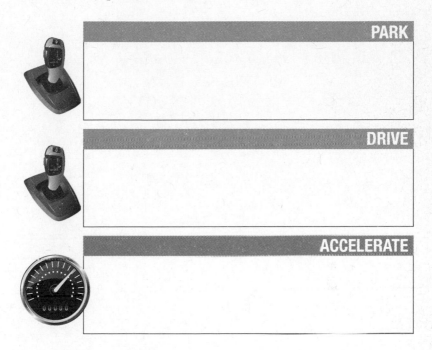

Extra effort is based on innovative ideas,
willingness to serve customers, and engagement
in work tasks. —James O'Toole

RESTART YOUR ENGINE

Every once in a while, a car battery dies and needs to be recharged. Maybe the engine hasn't been run in a while, or the weather has played a role. Or maybe it's not a problem with the battery. Maybe we're temporarily stalled in traffic or have taken our foot off the clutch a little too soon.

There are seasons in our lives, or temporary jams, which require us to restart our own internal batteries, or restart our engines. Maybe we sometimes lose our courage and, like a battery or engine block, we freeze up.

Not a day goes by that I don't pick up the paper and hear that XYZ Corporation is axing thousands of jobs, going into bankruptcy protection, or cutting its quarterly forecast. Most companies and households are re-examining their spending, and some are closing their wallets.

For a while, I tried to ignore the recession, but I've shifted my position. Now, I thank God for it. I embrace it because it has forced me to accelerate my efforts. The recession and all the changes going on around us have re-motivated me, restarted my engine, and they're doing the same for other businesses.

Here are some of the positive outcomes of the recession. It has:

- Motivated marketers to work their imaginations overtime to persuade consumers to part with precious dollars.

- Forced businesses to ask the tough questions, such as "Why are we doing this?"

- Jumpstarted work ethics—because, if you have a job, you are keenly aware that everything you do matters. The days of coming in for a chair, a check, and a coffee break are gone.

- Driven people to higher levels of productivity and performance in order to hang on to their jobs.

- Encouraged people to dig deep and make sure they are finding and creating value.

- Restarted and revved up engines everywhere!

People who restart their internal engines:

- Look at what they're going toward instead of what they're going through.

- Take the high road instead of living in the doldrums of disappointment.

- Shift their brilliance—create their own futures.

- Encourage themselves to keep moving forward.

So instead of cursing the recession, thank it. Say, "Thank you, recession, for waking me up to the fact that I can engage in my work as never before—that I can do everything in my power to not only ride out this time of economic uncertainty, but actually flourish in it."

How Do You Know When It's Time?

So, how do you know if it's time for you to shift? In the words of the song "The Gambler" by Kenny Rogers, "You got to know when to hold 'em, know when to fold 'em, know when to walk away and know when to run." In other words, we know we have to shift into drive to get moving. We know that sometimes we have to shift into reverse, to backtrack or get out of a tough spot. And we know that at times we need to idle a bit until the path is clear.

The most common question from my readers and audiences is whether they should shift and do something that feeds their passion when there are no guarantees, when they have a family to feed and bills to pay. This is the million-dollar question—that's for sure.

The question is not whether you *should* shift into following your passion. The real question is what do you *fear* about your future that is causing you to be presently stuck in neutral? This is a question that only you can answer. It boils down to how much or how desperately you want to shift into the unknown for who you will become instead of settling for where you are. It comes down to whether you want to yield to your Vujá dé and live your future in the present.

Stan's Story

Stan was stuck in a seemingly dead-end job. Although he's still in that job today, he says his life doesn't feel as hopeless. Stan was hired as a manager for a hospital to be groomed for a senior leadership role. He reported directly to the vice president, who was in transition and left shortly after Stan came on board. The budget would not allow the vice president to take Stan with him to the new department, and his replacement brought in her own senior leadership, thereby leaving Stan with no chance of upward mobility. He could have left the organization, but its mission was close enough to his heart that he decided to stay and persevere.

At first, Stan was angry. Naturally. But he managed to channel that anger into creative productivity. See, he always wanted to be a writer, but he never took the opportunity to pursue it as a career. In his teens, he wrote short stories and poems that were published, and he was hired as a staff music reviewer for a magazine published and distributed by a church.

So Stan shifted. In a matter of six months, he wrote and self-published his first book. Stan was able to find the courage to pursue a new career, one that leveraged his passion and took him down a completely new path. His life's purpose has gone from settling for mediocrity to having the desire to create a legacy of which he can be proud. By using his gifts and talents, he is inspiring others to live better lives and be better people. His new motto is, "Life is short. Make every moment count." Stan recalibrated and took control of the steering wheel of his life. He made his future present.

Some people ask me, "What do I do if I keep trying, improving, and growing, but I'm stuck in my job because of my boss/the company/some other constraint out of my control?" If you are in a situation you can't change, what you can change is how you choose to view it. Shift your perspective from feeling like a victim of circumstances to one where you choose to see your situation as one that is helping you to release your brilliance. Ask yourself, are there other departments that you could shift to that would celebrate you rather than just tolerate you?

Here's another example from one of my subscribers. We'll call her Tina. Tina wrote to me that she is in her forties and had been working in the same industry for fifteen years. She described herself as self-motivated and a happy, positive person. However, while there were days she loved what she did, there were other days she "got a sucker punch in the belly from senior management that she didn't see coming." Tina went on to explain that she didn't care for a lot of the treatment she had to endure, that while her team was great, many of the departments within the organization were extremely dysfunctional.

When I first received Tina's letter, I was at a loss for words. Yet, her comments got me thinking. I've certainly never meant to imply that when your job is in sync with your passion, every day is a walk in the park. I am extraordinarily blessed to be able to release my brilliance in a way that furthers my purpose. But that doesn't mean I function in a constant state of bliss. In any endeavor in life—work, relationships, family, faith—there will be both good days and bad days. The question is, which do you have more of?

As long as you experience more pleasure than pain, as seems the case with Tina, I'm not advocating that you leave your job. Instead, let me ask you a question or two: For the short-term, does that job serve a purpose in your life? Does it keep a roof over your head, food on the table, shoes on your feet? If so, then choose to "hire" your employer to fulfill that particular need in your life. When you have bad days or when management sucker-punches you in the gut, reframe the situation and see it as one you've chosen for this moment in time. Shift it. Will that be your chosen situation forever? Maybe not. But for today, it meets your immediate needs. Knowing that you choose this temporary situation makes it much easier to get out of bed in the morning and give 100% while you work toward your freedom.

That being said, when pain consistently outweighs the pleasure in your job, then it may be time to shift. If you can simply no longer find a way to get fired up about your current position, then make the choice to move on. Move on to another department, another company, another career. It just may not be advisable to leap today! You may have to plan, strategize, save some money, and perhaps get some additional education or training. Shifting can take time.

Simon T. Says... Change or be changed by change.

Shift Your Brilliance Today

Shifting your brilliance is, in essence, using a fresh set of eyes to see the same thing everyone else sees, but in a unique way and responding brilliantly as a result. In a marketplace crowded with competition, plagued by challenges, and ruled by change, taking a fresh approach is the only key to survival.

Shifts are happening all around us. And it's not just people and companies—it's large populations of people, even countries. It's happening on a global scale from Tunisia to Cairo's Tahrir Square and those who brought down Hosni Mubarak, as well as in Libya with the death of Moammar Gadhafi. You have to scratch your head and say, "What's going on?" Well, it could be summed up in one word—exposure. As a result of the 15-year-old World Wide Web—the Internet—people are witnessing in a nanosecond what freedom and democracy look like, and they're shaking their heads and saying, "Why not us?" and "Why not now?" They are no longer accepting death, poverty, starvation, and high unemployment as the norm of their society. Thanks to Twitter, the CNN of the 21st century, they are connecting and sharing. Shift baby...these young people see the future now!

Latin America's shift to brilliance is to become a middle-class society by improving the quality of schools and reforming public spending, according to *The Economist* magazine. They are well on their way, it seems, with 40 million Latin Americans out of a population of over 500 million having lifted themselves out of poverty over the past six years. They have survived global economic collapse by opening up their economies to trade, foreign investment, privatization, and deregulation. Leading this shift is Brazil, which has 15% of the world's oil reserves, a large stock of minerals, a quarter of the world's arable land, and 30% of its fresh water. In 2001, economist Jim O'Neill with Goldman Sachs coined the phrase "BRICS nations," which then included Brazil, Russia, India, and China, and now also includes South Africa. It is projected the BRICS nations will dominate world economic growth over the coming decades. These nations are implementing Vujá dé—seeing the future in the present—by addressing the core problems of low productivity, unequal income distribution, and widespread crime and violence. (Source: *The Economist*)

Don't wait on the future. Realize your possibilities today. Shift into what's waiting for you.

From time to time I like to introduce guest bloggers to all my social media relationships. I simply ask them to submit an article that can be posted online. I don't tell them what to write, I just remind them that if it doesn't move them then it won't move my audience either. Here is what I featured in a blog written by Gundala from Paris, France:

> I spent the past 21 years with the same corporation. It was a company that treated me well, gave me opportunities, and let me combine being a mother and wife while having an interesting job.
>
> I'm also a fervent reader of Simon's newsletters and books and at each thought or concept he shares I think to myself that what he shares feels "right." It's not new, earthshattering, or revolutionary. Just right.

And I realized through these readings that I had compromised myself into a job that was certainly interesting, but that didn't let me be brilliant. I was very good at my job, but didn't have fun with it anymore.

This was the starting point. Once I knew what felt wrong, I couldn't live with it anymore. Things had to change. And here is where my problem started! I knew what I wasn't brilliant at, but had no clue what I wanted to do with my life in order to shift.

And this is when something "magical" happened. Once I had decided that I wanted to be brilliant and to eventually quit my employer, the universe arranged itself around my mindset! Or did I just see doors I ignored before? Did I just start looking at the many possible roads before me, instead of focusing on a boring highway? Whatever it was, I was able to see it now.

A change was urgent and possible. It was like when you are in a dark room and somebody switches the light on and then off again. You will have seen what's in the room even if it's dark again. You can never "not know" again. So I moved along with my wish to create my future.

To cut a long story short, I am now self-employed, have published my first book and am in the process of finalizing two more books as I am writing this.

How did I find out that it was writing I wanted to get into? A combination of a lot of reflecting and feeling what I have most fun with. After several shortlists, the one item that stood out was "sharing knowledge." It simply makes me happy when I see how other people "get it," how they understand, comprehend, how they can see something that they haven't seen before, when they say "Ah!"

If it hadn't been for Simon, I would probably still be sitting at my desk waiting for something to happen. Here in Paris we call that déjà vu.

Now it's time to shift yourself and create the future.

A shift in your brilliance has come along to push you to ask profound questions. The first questions you must ask yourself are:

- *Where have I been? (An assessment of your experiences, education, and life journey)*

- *Why am I here? (A determination of what choices, decisions, and opportunities have brought you to this point)*

- *What can I do? (An assessment of what skills you will cultivate and grow)*

- *Where am I going? (An assessment of the snapshots that are flickering on the movie screen of your mind)*

Answering these questions is the initial step toward shifting from an average existence to brilliant living.

A new future is waiting to emerge for you and your business. You will experience a shift in your brilliance when you crack open the door of your mind and expose yourself to a fresh wind of new possibilities that were created in the midst of uncertainty.

The Ultimate Shifter

You might say I was raised on the altar of the Genesee Street Church of God in Buffalo, New York. My family had a favorite pew right up in the front, and every Sunday morning and

Wednesday evening I'd be there with them, praising the Lord in prayer and song. I loved that church. It was home to me. And even when I was away from the sacred sanctuary of that church, I was still surrounded by it.

I would often go to visit my grandmother (who recently went home to heaven), and she would tell me that she and her prayer partner had prayed for me every day of my life since I was born.

Well, her praying worked. I accepted Jesus Christ as my personal savior, and my life has never been the same again. He is the ultimate shifter.

My faith in God has sustained me in this "Shift Age." I am convinced that Jesus Christ is the answer for every problem that I will experience now and in the future.

Summary of the Seven Steps to Shift Your Brilliance

Step 1: See Differently

The first step in becoming a shifter is to see differently. What does it mean to see differently? It means to change your mindset. When you begin to see things differently, the opportunities before you change. To shift, you must be willing to change the scenery around you by examining everything you do and asking yourself if you are creating the tomorrow you want.

Step 2: Harness the Power of You, Inc.

The bottom line is that your organization wants the best from you. It wants employees who are assets (something of value) to the company rather than liabilities (disadvantages or drawbacks).

Your CEO must continually create value for and answer to stockholders, shareholders, and stakeholders who have a vested interest in your organization. The reason you face so much scrutiny at work is because Big Brother needs to know whether you are making the company money or costing it. That's why I strongly advise you to see yourself as a self-employed employee who is responsible for bringing value and productivity to the marketplace. Take control of your future by deploying your best thinking in growing yourself every day.

STEP 3: Ignite a Fresh Vision

Stale…stuck…spiritless. That is what an organization becomes when it loses its mojo! Simply launching a new product in this hypersensitive, over-communicative society isn't enough anymore. Opening a new building and hanging a sign out front is old and tired. Marketing to people through the "three screens"—television, computer, mobile phone—has lost its impact because people now have the power to immediately TiVo or delete you out of their space.

The moment customers interact with your organization, they will instantly judge if it is an authentic experience or the same old dry, dull, disjointed encounter. In their mind it's déjà vu all over again. Meanwhile, everyone inside the organization is waiting for sparks to fly and to be launched into the stratosphere. Yet in a few months' time, reality sets in and the brand "star" comes crashing back to earth. Why does this happen? Because too many organizations and leaders believe that reinvigorating with a new vision is a top-down rather than a bottom-up proposition. This leaves little room, if any, for a brilliant shift. It's up to you to ignite a fresh vision.

STEP 4: Fuel Your Mind

Once you have harnessed your courage and ignited a fresh vision, it's time to fuel your mind. If you are truly committed to shifting your brilliance, then you realize you must take responsibility for your own growth and development and unleash your potential. To shift in the right direction, you want to fill your mind with positive, productive thoughts, not useless, negative gossip or speculation.

STEP 5: Take the Wheel

To change the outside, look inside to see who's at the wheel. Taking the wheel starts with personal accountability. It's about taking responsibility for your own future, your own outcomes.

Ultimately, taking the wheel is about ownership. You are the operator of the vehicle that is your life. In fact, while there may be others along the way for encouragement and support, you are the only one who owns your future—and who can determine the next step in your journey.

STEP 6: Engage Your Gears

You have adopted a new way of seeing things, harnessed your inner strength, ignited your passion, fueled your mind, and taken the wheel. It's time now to engage those gears! Sometimes, though, when we attempt to shift, we can either grind a gear or slip out of a gear. When this happens, it's important to remember that making changes in our lives is often challenging.

STEP 7: Restart Your Engine

There are seasons in our lives, or temporary jams, which require us to restart our own internal batteries, or restart our engines. Maybe we sometimes lose our courage, and, like a battery or engine block, we freeze up. Take the initiative to find the keys to shift from average to brilliant.

RECOMMENDED READING LIST

Tons of books impacted me during my writing of *Shift Your Brilliance* and I just wanted to share a few with you.

The War of Art: Winning the Inner Creative Battle (Rugged Land, LLC, 2002) by Steven Pressfield. Steven demystifies and defines Resistance in such a powerful way that when you put his book down, you will stop making excuses for dreaming small.

Flash Foresight: How to See the Invisible and Do the Impossible (HarperCollins, 2011) by Daniel Burrus with John David Mann. I had lunch with Dan in La Jolla, California, when he was in the midst of writing his book. After spending half the day with him, my mind was stretched beyond my comfort zone. Oh my goodness, I felt that I had just been given a 21st century MBA in half a day.

Practically Radical: Not-So-Crazy Ways to Transform Your Company, Shake up Your Industry, and Challenge Yourself (HarperCollins, 2010) by William C. Taylor. Bill was one of the inspirations behind the original title of my book, *The Vujá dé Moment!* I was particularly drawn to this statement: "search for great ideas in unrelated fields, lift them out of the context in which they took shape, and shift them into your company."

Linchpin: Are You Indispensable? (Portfolio, 2010) by Seth Godin. Seth is one of the most incredible thought leaders on the planet.

Everything he writes pushes the boundaries of status-quo thinking and challenges you to escape the choke-hold of sameness. He makes the complex simple. For instance, he says, "A genius looks at something that others are stuck on and gets the world unstuck."

Powerpoints for Success (Whitaker House, 1997) by Bob Harrison. I am blessed to be able to call Bob a dear friend and mentor. With brilliant wit and wisdom, he reveals, through penetrating insights, pointed anecdotes, and heartwarming stories, the secrets and strategies of wildly successful people. He is America's Increase Activist, business owner, television personality, and an electrifying speaker.

Borrowing Brilliance: Six Steps to Business Innovation by Building on the Ideas of Others (Gotham Books, 2009) by David Kord Murray. I picked up this book and couldn't put it down. I was drawn to this statement: "Ideas are born out of other ideas, built on and out of ideas that came before." As a result, I saw his suggested reading list and decided that I needed to pay homage to the authors who had impacted me as I was writing *Shift Your Brilliance!*

Something You Should Know: The Fulfillment of Your Heart's True Desire (Four Star Books, 1919, and reprinted in 1993) by Clement Watt. This book is full of timeless wisdom. Watt taught his employees how to be uncommon workers. When he hired them, he would tell them, "I want you to learn to listen, to question, and to dream. Unlike those herded through the years of their existence like dumb, driven cattle, you must learn to question mediocrity, and give no quarter to dullness." Profound, to say the least.

The Happiness Advantage: 7 Principles of Positive Psychology That Fuel Success and Performance at Work (Crown Business, 2010) by Shawn Achor. A former Harvard Professor, Shawn shares his research of 1,600 Harvard students and dozens of Fortune 500 companies. His stories are riveting and full of advice on how to be happy with substance instead of fluff.

Empire State of Mind: How Jay-Z Went from the Street Corner to Corner Office (Portfolio/Penguin, 2011) by Zack O'Malley Greenburg. I have to admit I was intrigued by Jay-Z after seeing a photo of him on the cover of *Forbes* magazine with "Oracle of Omaha," Warren Buffet. Anyone who can go from an illegitimate hustle to a legitimate hustle and snag one of the prettiest women in the world, Beyonce, knows something I don't know.

Defy Gravity: Propel Your Business to High-Velocity Growth (Greenleaf Book Group, 2010) by Rebel Brown. Her name says it all. Her well-researched book gives you simple advice on how to achieve sustainable growth in today's volatile and precarious marketplace. It offers a superior level of knowledge built from her firsthand experiences in strategically positioning and launching more than 100 companies in twenty years.

Buy the Future: Learning to Negotiate for a Future Better than Your Present (Altar International, 2002) by Mensa Otabil. This man is one of the foremost global thought leaders on the planet. Here is just one nugget from him: "What we have today gives us the currency to purchase what will be tomorrow. Today's advantages must be used to buy tomorrow's opportunities." WOW, is that not priceless?

Visioneering: God's Blueprint for Developing and Maintaining Vision (Multnomah, 1999) by Andy Stanley. I first saw Andy twenty-five years ago while I was living in Atlanta, Georgia. He was a brilliant thinker back then, and he still is today. What he has done with leading the evangelical Christian church into the twenty-first century is simply amazing.

The Mackay MBA of Selling in the Real World (Portfolio/Penguin, 2011) by Harvey Mackay with a foreword by Lou Holtz. WOW... what can I say? I met Harvey, and after twenty minutes of talking with him he asked for my business card. Then he sent me an advance copy of this gem. I can't put it down. I have referenced it, retold stories from it, and can't wait for my children to start reading it.

Jewish Wisdom for Business Success: Lessons from the Torah and other Ancient Texts (Amacon, 2008) by Rabbi Levi Brackman and Sam Jaffe. I have a business advisor, Joel Novak, who I am blessed to have in my life. After reading this book, everything Joel ever told me or showed me finally clicked.

What You Think of Me Is None of My Business (Jove Books, 1979) by Terry Cole-Whittaker. I started reading this book and then noticed that I couldn't find it. I discovered that my wife had borrowed it, and she refused to give it back. Well, once I got it back I totally understood why my wife so enjoyed this direct, authentic discourse that makes readers stop and think.

Third World America: How Our Politicians Are Abandoning the Middle Class and Betraying the American Dream (Crown, 2010) by Arianna Huffington. She has her finger on the pulse of America and tracks the gradual demise of the nation as an industrial, political, and economic leader. Calling on the can-do attitude that is part of America's DNA, Huffington shows precisely what we need to do to stop our free fall and keep our country from turning into a Third World nation.

Dare to Be a Man: The Truth Every Man Must Know and Every Woman Needs to Know About Him (Berkley, 2009) by David G. Evans with foreword by T.D. Jakes. I read this book as I was entering my forties and feeling stuck, insignificant, and somewhat like a total wuss. This book helped me find my backbone voice. Just like the movie, *The Help*, this book reminded me that I am loved, I am brilliant, and I am special.

Three Feet from Gold: Turn Your Obstacles into Opportunities (Sterling with the Napoleon Hill Foundation, 2009) by Sharon L. Lechter and Greg S. Reid. This simple message packs a mighty punch in the gut. After you stand up again you will see what has always been there, but you will see it for the first time. It's totally Vujá dé.

Increase Your Financial IQ: Get Smarter with Your Money (Business Plus/Hachette, 2008) by Robert Kiyosaki. If you haven't read *Rich Dad Poor Dad,* then you have missed a gem of a story. Simply put, Robert is one of the foremost financial educators for the everyday man on the planet. Get every book he has ever written. Trust me on this one. His Vujá dé way of thinking will shift you.

Black Wall Street: From Riot to Renaissance in Tulsa's Historic Greenwood District (Eakin Press, 1998) by Hannibal B. Johnson. Early in the twentieth century, the black community in Tulsa—the "Greenwood District"—became a nationally renowned entrepreneurial center. It attracted pioneers from all over America who sought new opportunities and fresh challenges. Legal segregation forced blacks to do business among themselves. The key takeaway for me was seeing African-Americans actually believe in and support one another.

A Whole Mind: Why Right Brainers Will Rule the Future (Riverhead, 2006) by Daniel Pink. First of all, Daniel is one of the nicest people you could ever meet. I met him years ago when we were both speaking for the annual meeting of the National School Boards Association. I lent this book to a friend and never saw it again. I understand why. Daniel says, "The future belongs to a different kind of person with a different kind of mind: artists, inventors, storytellers—creative and holistic 'right-brain' thinkers whose abilities mark the fault line between who gets ahead and who doesn't."

Live Your Dream (Destiny Image, 2009) by Mark Chironna. God put this man in my path when I was full of potential but had no structure to exercise my gift. He is my master teacher and the person who has had the most profound impact on my life within the past 14 years. He is my mentor and spiritual father. I wrote my first book after listening to him for five years.

Character Matters (Charisma House, 2003) by Mark Rutland. When I first met Dr. Rutland, I knew I was in the presence of a giant thinker. The title says it all. Get everything he has ever written. He is brilliant.

A Hand to Guide Me: Legends and Leaders Celebrate the People Who Shaped their Lives (Meredith Books, 2006) by Denzel Washington with Daniel Paisner. This book was a gift from Clarence Otis, Chairman and CEO of Darden Restaurants. It showcases how the kindness of mentors has shaped the lives of legendary personalities. Best of all, a percentage of the proceeds benefits the Boys and Girls Clubs of America.

The Greatest Secret: God's Law of Attraction for Lasting Happiness, Fulfillment, Health, and Abundance in Life (White Stone, 2006) by Ron McIntosh. When I first met Ron at the suggestion of his brother Gary, I was blown away with his theological earthiness and substantive depth. I love Jesus, but his fan club sometimes freaks me out. Ron is one of the cool ones in the fan club. Get his book.

The Breakthrough Company: How Everyday Companies Become Extraordinary Performers (Crown Business, 2008) by Keith McFarland. Based on a five-year, 7,000 company study, McFarland highlights real-world tools and myth-busting insights that can be used by anyone wanting his or her business to join this exclusive circle.

Africa Rising: How 900 Million African Consumers Offer More than You Think (Wharton School Publishing, 2009) by Vijay Mahajan with Robert E. Gunther. Mahajan reveals this remarkable marketplace as a continent with massive needs and surprising buying power. He reveals how India and China are staking out huge positions throughout Africa and shows the power of the diaspora in driving investment and development.

ACKNOWLEDGMENTS

First of all, I would like to thank my wife and business partner, Renee, and my brilliant children, Daniel and Madison, for being the wind beneath my wings. I would like to thank Ellena Balkcom for her collaboration in the remix version of *Shift Your Brilliance* and Caroline Bartholomew for being my brilliant editor in pulling this brilliant work together. You are a joy to work with, and I am so happy that you agreed to be involved with this project. A very special thank you goes to DL Karl for being my brilliant thought partner. You are the best! And finally, thanks to my brilliant assistant, Melissa Spencer, for masterfully handling my schedule, which changes with the wind.

I have to thank Janet Goldstein and Elizabeth Marshall, who kindly did an 11th hour nip and tuck on the manuscript. I am forever grateful.

To Dr. Mark Chironna, thank you for telling me that you believed in me. I have waited 13 years to hear you say that, and you finally did. You can tell what God thinks about you based on the people who come into your life. He must really think I am something special. I can honestly say you have taught me, through your character, intellect, Italian Mafia street sense, and passion for God, how to be a man, husband, father, and provider. I love you.

Joel Novak, you taught me Jewish wisdom on how to do business. You showed up in my life when I was stuck in neutral and saw what I could become. You didn't give me a handout; you gave me a hand up. I will never forget the weekend Renee and I spent with you and Valerie in Bridgehampton. You were kind enough to drive me around The Hamptons and show me what was possible with a dream, a strategy, relationships, and hard work.

I am grateful to all the brilliant men and women who have left an imprint on the canvas of my mind and heart—Mark Sanborn, Joyce Meyer, Myles Munroe, Larry Lynch, Jim Lewis, Al Weiss, Linda Fareed, Tom Hill, Jim & Naomi Rhode, Nido Qubein, Thom Winniger, Valerie Ferguson, Willie Jolley, Bob Harrison, Tudor Bismark, Sam Chand, Dale Bronner, Walter Bond, The Fab Four, The ESN Group, Scott Friedman, Genevieve Bos, Brian Palmer, Desi Williamson, the late great Keith Harrell, the late great John Alston, and the rest of the NSA family.

Finally, I extend my thanks to all the speakers' bureaus that believed in me when I left Disney...when I didn't know yet if I would make it.

ABOUT THE AUTHOR

SIMON T. BAILEY is a Leadership Catalyst who aspires to inspire 10% of the world's population to find their passion and release their brilliance. He equips individuals and organizations with practical tools and solutions. He provides actionable takeaways that go beyond feel-good content and produce sustainable results. His insights are based on his work with 1,000 organizations on six continents.

After working as Sales Director at the world-renowned Disney Institute, Simon founded Brilliance Institute, which designs and delivers its own proprietary curriculum for personal and professional development. The results of this work are increased productivity, personal accountability, customer retention, and good old-fashioned happiness.

MeetingNet.com selected him as one of the Editors Favorite Speakers which put him in the same category with Thomas Friedman. *Meeting & Conventions* magazine cited him as one of the best keynote speakers ever heard or used. This puts him in the same category with Bill Gates, General Colin Powell, and Tony Robbins.

Simon has impacted the lives of more than one million people with his counsel and coaching from the C-Suite to the front lines for clients including Verizon, Chevron, Nationwide, Society of Human Resource Management, and The Conference Board with his forward-thinking, practical, interactive sessions and action-oriented programs.

Recently, Harrison College, based in Indianapolis, Indiana, USA, and founded in 1911, has partnered with Simon to create professional development content for its corporate partnerships.

He is also a columnist for *American City Business Journal.* His weekly article appears in 43 markets and reaches 11 million unique visitors to their websites.

Simon was named one of the Top 25 Hot Speakers shaping his profession by *Speaker* magazine. He is a Certified Speaking Professional (CSP). CSP is the speaking profession's international measure of speaking experience and skill. Fewer than 10% of speakers globally hold this designation.

Simon is a graduate of Rollins College Executive Management Program, one of the top 25 best private graduate business schools in the USA. He holds a Master's Degree from Faith Christian University and was inducted as an honorary member of the University of Central Florida Golden Key International Honor Society.

Simon and his family reside in a small quaint town of 2,500 residents and a few dirt roads in Windermere, Florida, USA, where he works on his tan year round.

EDUCATIONAL RESOURCES FROM
SIMON T. BAILEY AND BRILLIANCE INSTITUTE, INC.

Sign up for my free weekly brilliance newsletter—
www.simontbailey.com

Simon's blog:
www.simontbailey.com/blog

Building Business Relationships by Simon T. Bailey—
7 Day Free Trial www.lynda.com/trial/SimonTBailey

Follow me:
www.twitter.com/simontbailey

Simon's YouTube channel:
www.youtube.com/simontbailey

Link with Simon T. Bailey:
www.linkedin.com/in/simontbailey

Become a Fan of Simon T. Bailey—
https://www.facebook.com/SimonTBrillionaire

Download the Simon T. Bailey App at
www.simontbailey.com

Request the free e-book, *Meditate on Your Personal Brilliance,* by
e-mailing hello@simontbailey.com

eBooks by Simon T. Bailey

Simon Says Dream: Live a Passionate Life—This was the first book I released when I left Disney. Serena and Venus Williams were some of the first celebrities to read it. http://ow.ly/qljPZ

Success is an Inside Job—I wrote this book from a deep place and really had to live it. In other words, I had to live it from the inside out. http://ow.ly/qljSG

Meditate on Your Professional Brilliance—These are pithy one liners and sound bites that will help you get through the day. http://ow.ly/qljUP

Brilliant Service is the Bottom Line—Everything I learned from Disney and from working with over 1,000 organizations— everything I discovered about the awesomeness of customer experience—is included in this book. http://ow.ly/qljXF

Meditate on Your Personal Brilliance—This was written out of my struggle with wanting to know how to shift my thinking and live a meaningful life. http://ow.ly/qlk31

For More Information

To inquire about having Simon T. Bailey speak at your next meeting:

Please e-mail hello@simontbailey.com

Website—www.simontbailey.com

Connect with Simon T. Bailey

Twitter—@simontbailey

Facebook—Simon T. Bailey

LinkedIn—Simon T. Bailey